THE
SATANIC
PHILOSOPHER

REV. CAIN

This is a work of religious nature, and the information herein is intended solely for educational purposes.

You are responsible for yourself, your actions, and how you conduct yourself as a human being – not us, and not anyone else.

Act responsibly, and conduct yourself in a way that exemplifies honor, integrity, and decency towards yourself and those around you.

I dedicate this manuscript to the students of the

Left-Hand Path – with this book, may your

lives, souls, and studies flourish forevermore in

the embered light and grace of our

Lord Satan – within his

kingdom, you are

free.

AUTHOR'S PREFACE

This manuscript – *The Satanic Philosopher* – has been an ongoing-yet-intermittent effort of mine for the past five years. In this span of time, all manner of tragedy has found me: my father recently passed away in a *terrible* motorcycle accident; my mother was nearly killed; my health has suffered in many ways that I am still recovering from; I have walked the path of solitude – bloodily, weak, and bereft of light. Yet, I am still here – I have persisted through some of the *worst* atrocities that life could besiege a human being with – and I have my faith to thank.

I have found success, failure, tragedy, triumph – in every way, I have been tested to an exhausting and *ruthless* extent – as a man, a partner, an author, and a religious leader. No stone has been left unturned in my mind or body, and I have been forced to face *every* fear, mentality, pathology, and bad habit that has stunted my growth – internally and externally.

The past half-decade of my life has demanded me to meet Herculean expectations – and, admittedly,

I questioned at times if I had the strength to endure the cataclysmic sorrows that life was heaping upon my weary shoulders. At any moment, I could have chosen to drop the weight – to *refuse* the suffering, pain, and agony that life was unfairly demanding I carry to no discernible end – and no clear-minded soul would have *dared* fault me for giving up. But I did not – in fact, I have *prospered* in the wake of the torrents of tragedy that have swept through my life, because I realized and accepted that there was no sense or respite in letting myself be consumed by the tragedies of life. What would it solve? How would I alleviate my pain by surrendering to every terrible reality tormenting me? I realized that there was no respite waiting – there was no lifeboat, and there was no redemption unless **I** decided to strive for that redemption – so, I did exactly that. I picked myself up and began to heave myself through the smog and darkness of life towards a horizon that I *knew* would offer me the strength that I needed to weather life's cruel tempests: our kingdom of Hell.

As I write these words, I have sacrificed just about one-third of my *entire* life to writing on behalf of our Lord Satan – it has been, is, and will *always* be my life's purpose, and I will continue to spread the good word of the Devil until the day I die. I believe that what I am doing is noble, and *necessary* – this world has been deprived of the power that Hell can offer humankind, because it has been blinded and deceived by that craven Christ and his father, God.

There exists no focus, pursuit, or dream in my life more meaningful than my quest to heal the world's disfigured perceptions of traditional Satanism – to address and heal *centuries* of unopposed derision, hyperbole, fear, prejudice, and condemnation from an intolerant world that persecutes *everything* that it does not understand. As traditional Satanists, we are amongst the most misjudged, abominated, and disparaged practitioners of **any** religion that has or will ever preach upon God's green Earth – and the reason for this discrimination is nothing more than the discomfort, fear, and bigotry of our neighbors.

The narrative of the past two thousand years is that traditional Satanism is a toxic seedbed for cruelty, violence, human rights violations, and unrepentant depravity – that Satanism is a source of *sickness* in an otherwise unsick world and we, as celebrants of

Satan, *must* be cast out from the god-fearing cities, cul-de-sacs, and suburbs. I argue the contrary – the Devil is the antidote to the sickness of *Christianity* that has spread like an inextinguishable inferno for millennia, needlessly snuffing out *millions* of lives for no reason other than our refusal to surrender to and obey the tyrannical rule of God – it is pathetic.

Though it is true that Satanism *does* have its share of seedy practitioners just like any other faith, they are the exception – **not** the standard. I believe that much of the darkness afflicting our faith of theistic Satanism comes from the outside world – from the sycophants of God, the agnostics with a Napoleon complex, and the atheistic Satanists that deride our religion. As well, I blame those who, for *centuries,* have bastardized the imagery, beliefs, history, and hyperbole that surrounds our faith in order to fuel their malicious agendas – the types of people who commit violent acts and then blame the Devil, like Richard Ramirez; the media story-spinners and the fear-mongering masses that have orchestrated and fueled hysteria, like the Satanic Panic of the 1980s; the soccer mom at the grocery store who does not understand Gothic subculture, but is *confident* that the teenager across the aisle is a good-for-nothing devil worshipper – it is all just one big joke at our religion's expense, and **nobody** has made a decent attempt to address it – until now, with *The Satanic Philosopher* and the efforts of The Infernal Circle.

It is no simple task to teach the world the nature of a religion – *especially* when that religion has been the victim of unrelenting derision, misinformation, and persecution for *centuries* – but I did not choose to take on this endeavor because I thought it would be easy. I was well aware from the very beginning that my endeavor to restore our faith of traditional Satanism would prove to be inconsolably difficult, painful, unnerving, and at times, feel *impossible* to achieve – but I knew that it was necessary, so there was no discomfort frightening enough to dissuade me from continuing forward. If it was not me, then who would it be? How many more years, decades, and *centuries* would pass before someone else was willing to shoulder the grueling task of repairing a religion that has been neglected for the better part of more than two *thousand* years? It **had** to be me, and every day that passes, I am thankful to myself for having the courage and strength of mind to pick up this *extremely* arduous-yet-rewarding chance to change the world for the better, and leave my mark on the history of our faith of traditional Satanism.

Though I believe it is a noble undertaking, there is no doubt in my mind that this endeavor will remain *incredibly* challenging – in a world that is tethered to the vacuous heart of God, who would dare listen to the insights of a Satanic minister? Who amongst the god-fearing masses would dare stray from their medieval superstitions and confess that they have been misled in their beliefs surrounding Satanists? Our religion has become the world's default "pin the tail on the Devil" patsy for *anything* the masses do not have a concrete answer to, and it shall take a *tremendous* amount of work on my behalf to peel away the cataracts of God that have kept blind the world for over two thousand years – but I am ready to take on this challenge for I *know* I shall succeed.

With *The Satanic Philosopher*, I shall forever alter the landscape of not only traditional Satanism, but the world as a whole – even if I were to trudge this mortal Earth for another century, I believe that *The Satanic Philosopher* will go down in history as my magnum opus contribution to traditional Satanism. Though I have already reached great strides in my pursuit to repair our religion's fetid reputation, this book will catapult me *lightyears* closer to realizing my goal – though, of course, this goal is **not** static.

There *is* no endpoint – no statistic, sales figure, or achievement that would lead me to say, "okay, our religion is fixed – there is nothing more that I can do." My effort to repair traditional Satanism is not a goal with a predetermined stopping point – there is no finale. There are no fixed criteria by which I would be able to say that I have achieved my goal to heal our faith – it is an *ongoing* accomplishment that builds with every book I sell, every page that is read, and every soul that feels empowered by my words. The change that I wish to see in our religion will **not** take place in one fell swoop of *immediate* change, but in the gradual chipping away of the silt and grime and filth that has entombed our faith for the past two thousand years – with *every* life that I positively impact, and with every superstition that I help to abolish, our religion will be strengthened.

The restoration of our religion begins, is furthered, and ends by improving the lives of individuals – of critics and celebrants alike, and those who wish to understand the *true* nature of traditional Satanism. With *The Satanic Philosopher*, that is what I offer you – the world's most powerful, comprehensive, and illuminating treatise on our faith of traditional Satanism that has or will ever be authored. In *The Satanic Philosopher,* you shall find an astonishing wealth of insight into the inner workings and long-forgotten realities of our faith – our beliefs, values, opinions, motivations, and too, the philosophy that breathes life into the lungs of traditional Satanism.

As you explore *The Satanic Philosopher*, I ask that you do so with an open mind, a heart inspired, and a genuine desire to learn – this book shall offer you an *unparalleled* cornucopia of knowledge, but this knowledge will prove worthless unless it is used in a way that empowers your life or the lives of those around you. As I touch on throughout *The Satanic Philosopher* – amassing knowledge for the sake of having it is a fool's errand, and it will lead to **zero** growth as a person or as a Satanist. The only value of knowledge is in its potential – in how it is used to change and reshape reality in a way that leads to significant, positive growth. There is no amount of knowledge on Earth or in Hell that will bring value to your life unless **you** have committed to applying that knowledge in a productive and noble manner.

As a traditional Satanist in a world that is ruled by the lambs of God, it is *your* responsibility to create the life you wish to live – nobody will provide you with the strength, autonomy, wealth, or knowledge that you believe you deserve – you are celebrant of Satan, and you will be given no breaks or shortcuts in this monstrous world. Thankfully, in your hands and in your spirit, you have *every* tool you need to create the life that you desire – with the knowledge offered by *The Satanic Philosopher*, and with your unyielding faith as a traditional Satanist, your life is but clay to be reshaped by your will and design.

– Rev. Cain
Salem, MA

TO THE REVERED DEVILS OF PERDITION.

BY THE UNHALLOWED GRACE OF SATAN,

ILLUMINATED AND GLORIOUS SHEPHERD OF FIRE.

REVEREND CAIN WISHES GLORY, HEREIN, UNTO
THE BLACKENED FIELDS OF HELL.

Endless were the fruits of Satan, our Infernal Lord
in fire – the unholy powers bestowed upon us, the
horned children of his glorious kingdom of Hell.

When first he descended before us, upon a chariot
of cindered ash, enlightenment befell us – and our
souls found power through the light of darkness.

In Satan's reviled name, I honor the path that waits
ahead, paved with sulfur and fire – lead me to your
nectarous groves and the eternal kingdom of Hell!

THE INFERNAL DEDICATORY

As Satan fills our souls with fire, we shall know of his infernal grace – he shall shepherd us, and guide us through the darkling night of immortal devilry.

And with his sulfuric touch, we may feel the divine ichor of devils fill and flood our hearts – our atria, set afire with the gilded gloom of Satan's godhood.

Through his deliverance, we shall know him as the sovereign light, and savior – our crusader sheathed in the ever-burning flames of our kingdom of Hell.

THE NAMES AND ORDER

OF ALL THE

INFERNAL TENETS AND DOCTRINES

21

THIS BOOK BELONGS TO

_____

INTRODUCTION

In my blackest hours, I have turned time and time again to our faith of traditional Satanism – when I have felt weak, I have found strength in the Devil's word; in moments of *impossible* sorrow, my spirit has been replenished by the fires of Hell; when the light has ebbed and waned from my feverish eyes, the grace of our Lord Satan spirited me once more with vigor, purpose, and pride – at every twist and turn of life, the Devil has brought me the strength necessary to not only survive, but to *thrive* amidst the unrelenting chaos of this brutal, desolate Earth.

My faith as a traditional Satanist has been the light to guide me out of the darkest moments that, many times, I did not believe I could survive – things that few people ever escape from, yet I managed to all because of the lessons, values, and mentality that I have learned from a decade of serving as a minister of our kingdom of Hell. The power and strength to be reaped from the religion of traditional Satanism are *remarkable* – but few people would ever think of our religion as a wellspring of positive growth, endurance, and empowerment, thanks to over two thousand years of the lambs of God spreading their unopposed hysteria, propaganda, and superstition.

With *The Satanic Philosopher*, I hope to offer you the same degree of comfort and confidence in our faith that has helped *me* endure the wicked winters of life for the past decade and counting. In order to achieve this, I will analyze, demystify, and explain *countless* superstitions, hyperboles, myths, stories, assumptions, and prejudices that have afflicted our faith for the past two millennia – and in their place, I shall leave you with accurate, *applicable* ways of thinking that shall better not only your life, but the lives of those around you and the world as a whole.

I believe that it is long, *long* overdue for traditional Satanism to reclaim its seat of nobility, and to shed the shackles of disparagement and derision that the world has placed upon us – it sickens me, watching the masses pretend as if traditional Satanism is *full* of the delusional, the childish, the violent, and the malevolent. Our religion is a source of *remarkable* strength, poise, clarity, knowledge, and unyielding resilience – if you require evidence to back up my assertion, think of the fact that the *entire* world has been out to exterminate our religion for more than two thousand years, and not only are we *still* here, but we are more powerful and enlivened than ever.

That is what traditional Satanists do – we survive, endure, and prosper in the face of adversity. We do not surrender to the cruelty of life – we *persist*, for our livelihood does not depend on a world that has for thousands of years reviled us based on nothing more than the grounds of conjecture and medieval superstition. That said, I believe it is still *necessary* for the aforestated superstitions to be put to rest so that our religion may be clearly understood by the curious and contemptuous alike – those that might be interested in becoming Satanists should have an unadulterated idea of what to anticipate, and those that revile us should at least base their hysteria off of the truth instead of spooky stories, like children.

With *The Satanic Philosopher*, I shall address and abolish as many of these superstitions as I possibly can – no longer shall the hysteria of the world feed upon the blood of Satanism like a bloated, *pathetic* tick. So long as breath still fills my mortal lungs, I will **not** sit idly by and watch the continued decline of our religion – the derision, hyperbole, prejudice, and *baseless* censure spat from the spaded tongues of the god-fearing masses. I will not look from afar as traditional Satanism rots in the pious hands of a world that has seemingly unified in the pursuit of our ruination. We *will* endure, because that is what traditional Satanists have always done – and *The Satanic Philosopher* will light the way forward for you, me, and *millions* of wayward souls that wish to discover the true nature of traditional Satanism.

THE EGO'S TYRANNY

I believe that the soul of Satanism is dead and what stands atop its grave is nothing more than a dreary caricature – a poor man's parody of what our faith *once* represented – wisdom, nobility, strength, and unwavering devotion to our Lord Satan. What now exists in the 21st century is, in my eyes, little more than an imitation – a tongue-in-cheek charade that loosely attempts to remain accurate, though *mostly* cares about shocking the world, feeling rebellious, and making a quick dollar off of the Devil's name.

Our faith has become a superficial boogeyman – a soulless abomination that appears to revere its own infamy more than it does the values or philosophy of Satanism itself – and this has contributed just as much to the decay of our religion over the past two *thousand* years as Christian persecution. I believe that *countless* Satanists have played a vital role in the desecration of our religion – though the world has condemned and assailed us from the *outside*, it is not to blame for the *internal* disharmony that can be noticed within Satanism. The lambs of God are **not** responsible for the posturing, cruelty, rampant egoism, and self-aggrandizing theatrics that spread like wildfire within our faith – how could they be?

We cannot justly point the finger at Christians, the Pope, or the Vatican and use them as scapegoats to avoid accepting responsibility for the role we have played in our ruination – after all, that M.O. is that of the god-fearing souls, **not** Satanists. If we are to heal the faith of Satanism as a whole, then we *must* address our possible complicity in the decay of our religion – we cannot begin to heal our faith until a concerted effort is made to address and resolve the ways in which *we* might be preventing its healing.

I believe that Satanism has decayed into a ghastly, *unrecognizable* imitation of itself – a blind horror, clawing at its own clay while pointing with blame at the rest of the world, possessed by its delusions and ignorant to the fact it is devouring itself – like a dying Ouroboros that cannot see its mortality, yet continues to consume itself because it believes that it is sempiternal. We are **not** indestructible, nor are we impervious from feeling on an individual level the repercussions of tarnishing the values, beliefs, and integrity of Satanism – in fact, we can already *clearly* see this ripple effect of neglect taking place in every corner, crevice, and alleyway of our faith.

Our religion *once* exemplified strength, refusing to participate in the senseless drama and theatrics that most of the world is enslaved by – wanton cruelty, petty quarrelling, ignorance, self-aggrandizement, xenophobia, paranoia – the attributes and behavior that I would expect to find amongst the masses of God but that I have *also* begun to notice within our faith of Satanism – traditional and atheistic, alike.

Since the dawn of Christianity and the consequent birth of Satanism, the purpose of our faith has been to serve as the antithesis of God and his lambs – to exemplify and uphold the values of our Lord Satan in defiance of a crusaderist world that *demands* we pledge fealty to the tyrannical reign of God. There was a time when the whole of Satanism embodied the values of our Lord Satan – his strength, clarity, *justified* rebellion, wisdom, and self-mastery – not the frailty, malice, or derision that I believe is now synonymous with *either* path of our ailing religion.

Over the centuries, *countless* factors have abetted the ruination of Satanism as a whole – superstition, prejudice, unbridled egos, a lack of leadership, and the contempt of an *entire* world, just to name a few of the most pressing matters working against us. It may be an unpopular opinion of mine, but I believe there is another, more damaging factor that has not only undermined the integrity of Satanism, but has gone almost *entirely* unacknowledged: the neglect and abandonment of traditional Satanism in favor of atheistic Satanism. What happens when a living organism is left to its own devices – bereft of what it needs to survive and thrive? What happens to the water that for too long stands still, or the fruit that tries to grow amidst the midsummer humidity? All living things, once neglected and abandoned, shall be seized by the rotting reclamation of Pestilence.

A religion *cannot* be healthy in part – the whole of it must be held to equal standards, without turning a blind eye to the Pestilence spreading through oft-neglected shadows – if you do not believe me, take a look at how low the Church has plunged from its so-called ideals. For *centuries*, it has cherrypicked its way through untold controversies, catastrophes, and crimes against humanity, and now decay is the only substance that lies behind the gilded façade it presents to the world. It is a rotten, vapid caricature of the principles it alleges to promote, and we must take a lesson from how it has disfigured itself – we *cannot* allow Satanism to succumb to this dire fate.

Once a religion makes excuses for deviating from its own messages and tenets, the religion ceases to be a trustworthy source of knowledge or power for the world. There is something *deeply* insidious and disquieting about a religion that refuses to practice what it preaches – who are you to lecture the world about how it should live if you cannot follow your own advice? As a preacher, ministry, or messenger of *any* religion, your message stops being valuable and starts being dictatorial the *moment* you realize that you are not adhering to the values, limitations, and philosophy that you are trying to sell to others.

Okay, so we know that there are more problems to deal with than the cruelty of God's cronies – what do we do next? What are the *specific* problems that we should address, in order to stop contributing to the ruination of our religion? Well, there are issues of *all* shapes, sizes, and severity, but I believe that most of them can be collated into two overarching problems to address: traditional Satanism's lack of leadership and how Satanists mistreat one another.

You might be wondering why it matters at all that traditional Satanism has lacked leadership – and I will tell you why. As I stated previously, a religion *cannot* be healthy in part – the whole of it must be held to equal standards, lest rot begins to seep into those parts left neglected in favor of the new, shiny addition to the religion. Since traditional Satanism is the foundation of all Satanism, to neglect it is to forsake everything built on top of that now-rotted foundation – which includes *atheistic* Satanism. If traditional Satanism had been caretaken and given effective leadership, it would not have deteriorated so grievously – *especially* over the past century, as atheistic Satanism arose in place of traditionalism.

While there have arisen a few honorable figures in the *atheistic* realm of Satanism, *traditionalism* has suffered without an estimable authority for as long as I can recollect – I would wager centuries, at this point. Though it sounds like showboating, I do not believe any *single* person or body has contributed as much to traditional Satanism as I have – and, for this reason alone, I regard myself as the leadership that for so long traditional Satanism has direly and *desperately* needed. There shall come a time when other potential leaders and authorities will arise for traditional Satanism – but, until then and as history shall remember – Reverend Cain saved traditional Satanism from an unceremonious, untimely grave.

Well, that solves *one* of the two overarching issues that I believe should be addressed – but what about the other? What about the wickedness, cruelty, and revilement that is so often shared between atheistic and traditional Satanists? Over the past decade that I have served as a minister of Hell, I have observed firsthand the sobering extent of how disappointing and *disgusting* person-to-person interaction can be amongst Satanists of varying beliefs – atheistic vs. traditional, regarding each other as mortal enemies as they demonstrate behavior and xenophobia that, quite honestly, reminds me of Christians – and for what? It is truly disturbing to see the blindness and arrogance of some Satanists – those that condemn, persecute, and ridicule their kinsmen of a different subsect of the *same* religion, then blame Christians and the outside world for **all** of the oppression that they must unjustly suffer – never *once* stopping to consider the fact that they may have contributed to their suffering, and they, *too*, are guilty of tyranny. I believe that traditional and atheistic Satanists are equally guilty of this hideous behavior, but in their own uniquely contemptible ways – I shall address them now, and I will not sugarcoat any ugly truths.

While I bear no animosity in my heart towards our atheistic counterparts, I believe many narratives of ill-will and derision originate from their side of the fence – narratives that *cannot* continue, if there is to ever be a unification of Satanists or the mending of our religion. We must not disaffect one another, nor fuel the division of our already-fractured faith in order to cater to or coddle gluttonous egos – this goes for *both* atheistic Satanists and traditionalists.

On countless occasions, I have witnessed atheistic Satanists cast the first stones of conflict, usually in a pompous spectacle, as they mock and spit venom upon a traditionalist for their "mythological" faith, *completely* oblivious to the fact that **their** religion would not exist without traditional Satanism – that Satanism was born from Christianity, and that we would have no concept of Satan without the Bible.

A misperception exists amongst atheistic Satanists that traditional Satanism is child's play – a religion for the juvenile and those that adhere to mythology rather than objective truth – that we are misguided, delusional, and unworthy to stand beside atheistic Satanists or call ourselves "true" Satanists. I argue the contrary – traditional Satanism is the heart and origin of this religion, and I believe it is time that we stop pretending otherwise – no amount of lying to ourselves and covering our ears to the truth shall dethrone traditional Satanism as our genesis faith.

I say this not with damnation or condemnation for atheistic Satanism – rather, it is the *genuine* belief that I hold after a decade of experience as a Satanic minister. It would be untrue and irrational of me to suggest that *every* atheistic Satanist believes in the aforesaid narrative regarding traditional Satanism, or that the whole of atheistic Satanism is belittling, persecutive or malicious in nature – that is *far* from the case. That said, I have experienced firsthand a *staggering* number of atheistic Satanists claim that

41

traditional Satanism is a laughable superstition and that the only "true" Satanism is atheistic Satanism.

I do not solely attribute blame to atheistic Satanists for the problems that plight our faith – I have seen *countless* traditional Satanists initiate meaningless and inexcusable conflict with atheistic Satanists to nurture their delicate egos. Interestingly, when this happens, it is usually related to the *same* ridiculous reason that atheistic Satanists use to disparage and deride traditionalists – a false sense of superiority, and the belief that *their* Satanism is the "real one." The atheistic Satanist ridicules the traditionalist by insisting their beliefs are little more than fairytales, and the traditionalist believes that, because theism came first, atheistic Satanism is not a real religion.

I think it really is quite embarrassing, all of it – the back-and-forth antagonizing and juvenility that we allow to persist in and defile our religion – the sort of *desperate*, schoolyard antics that I would expect to see amongst the god-fearing masses – **not** those that allege to live by the values, ethics, principles, and philosophy of Satanism. I could not give a shit less which side of the fence you are on – traditional or atheistic Satanism – we *both* matter, and we are *both* instrumental in the repairing and empowering of our faith. We must no longer abet the senseless division and destruction of Satanism – neither side of our faith is superior to the other, and this pissing contest *must* finally end – there is no other option.

That said, over the course of my tireless journey as a Satanic minister, few things have shocked me the way person-to-person interaction and segregation has within Satanism – it is akin to watching a black pit full of rabid animals devour each other without consideration of the bigger picture, blind and deaf to the world around them, never realizing that they are fighting an imagined enemy in a causeless war.

It is our obligation to repair Satanism, and we must begin this process by looking inwards – improving ourselves as human beings and practitioners as we pave a new, *unfractured* way forward for our faith, towards a sanctuary where each practitioner views the next as an equal and we may *all* concentrate on our growth – unimpeded, and without persecution. The whole of Satanism cannot be fixed and refined until each practitioner takes accountability for how

they represent our religion out in the world – once this becomes the "new normal," Satanism shall see rampant growth the likes of which has *never* been seen, therein ushering forth the New Age of Satan.

There is only so much that I can do myself – I can offer you all the insight in the world, but only *you* can apply it. It is the responsibility of a religion's worshippers to exemplify the values, philosophy, and principles *of* said religion – virtues, messages, morals, and lectures are worthless on paper unless they are pulled from the ink and applied in the real world – and this is what I hope to achieve with *The Satanic Philosopher*. With this book, I offer every reader an infallible wealth of knowledge that they may use to create *remarkable* change – in life, the world as a whole, and in our religion of Satanism.

THE ROAD AHEAD

Our infamous manuscript both praised and reviled, *The Infernal Gospel*, is a world-renowned bible for traditional Satanism – a thorough-yet-introductory exploration of the old-world ways of this religion, meant to educate and inspire those new to its path. It is a looking glass that reveals the lost origins and disregarded truths of Satanism – its history, nature, celebrations, philosophies, ethics, sins, and what it means to embrace the old ways – to be a traditional Satanist and devote oneself to the kingdom of Hell.

As well, within the depths of *The Infernal Gospel,* you shall find the *Infernal Tenets* – five guidelines for self-rule that I created to help practitioners act in accord with the values, beliefs, and philosophy of traditional Satanism. The Satanist that embraces these tenets shall *flourish* both in everyday life and in their Satanic worship upon the Left-Hand Path.

The Infernal Tenets strive to refine one's character and strip them of self-destructive thought patterns, ideologies, and behaviors that may pose a threat to their unrealized potential. If *fully* embraced, these five tenets will create a tougher, braver, wiser, and more resilient person that is capable of weathering the storms of life – a person who will **always** come out on the other side of conflict stronger than they went into it – they will become *truly* indestructible.

I first began conceptualizing the Infernal Tenets in my early days of studying demonology and rites of exorcism – at this time in my life, I was still toying with the thought of enrolling in seminary school to become a holy priest of God and Heaven on Earth, expelling Satan and his legions from the good and "guiltless" souls of your average, ordinary people.

There has always burned a fire, within me – a great flame and calling that, when followed, has led me time and time again to the gates of Hell – before I began preparing for priesthood, I was *inconsolably* disturbed by this realization. It led to many restless nights wrought by terror and curiosity as I mused over the bigger picture at play and what in Hell's name it could *possibly* mean or have to do with me. Once I became interested in exorcism and the idea of becoming a priest, the internal compass that had always pointed towards Hell *finally* made sense to me – I was being called to rid the world of Satan's legions and the stain of his influence so that I may protect the beauty, hope, and sanctity of the human soul. This belief brought me peace for a few years, but it would eventually reveal itself as an illusion.

While theology and religion were always topics of interest for me, something felt disingenuous about my decision to pursue priesthood – but, since I did not know where to begin reconsidering my beliefs and motives, I continued in my studies and ignored the rising sense of dread that dragged from my soul like an anchor of augury. As I would come to learn shortly thereafter, try as you might, you shall *never* outrun or outsmart Fate – she **will** always find you.

On one particularly dreary and foreboding October night more than a decade ago, an incident occurred that forced me to confront that lingering feeling of unease – though I will not waste more pages of *The Satanic Philosopher* with tales from my formative years, I will say that this incident was the defining moment that replotted the course of my soul from Heaven to Hell – though I could not have possibly known it at the time, this event would permanently change my life, the world, and Satanism – *forever*.

In the aftermath of this event, I began *obsessively* devouring *every* resource at my disposal regarding the topics of demonology, occultism, Hell, and the role that Satan has played both in our world and in the Abrahamic faiths. Before I knew it, my chance to enroll in seminary school had passed me by, and now I was thinking more often of Satan than I was of God – an omen of many infernal things to come.

As I poured over ancient tome after ancient tome, soaking up wisdom into the cerulean hours of each morning, I came to a realization that both shocked and *invigorated* me – Satan's side of the story was more honorable and gallant than that of God's, and I no longer viewed myself as a protestor of Satan's reign. Satan's story was *fearless*, and virtuous, and spoke to the most bestial part of my heart as a man.

In the weeks following this discovery, I would not only forsake my Christian upbringing, but I would begin an *exhaustive* period of introspection – time crawled to a stop, and every day became a vicious pursuit of self-examination as I questioned myself and how I could have *possibly* ended up in such an unusual spiritual and philosophical quandary – the aspiring exorcist-turned-sympathizer of Satan, led far, *far* astray from the seraphic path of priesthood.

For the first time in my life, I had *clearly* heard the calling that since childhood's earliest hour had led me to the doorstep of Hell – only now, I knew that my mission was different and that I would become an emissary of Satan's godship – not an adversary, nor another spineless decrier of his alleged cruelty against humanity. I had heard this bullshit story *far* too often during both my Christian upbringing and my clerical studies, and I knew that it was nothing more than an unsubstantiated claim for the masses to regurgitate out of fear, ignorance, and prejudice.

With this revelation, I began to search for and read *every* modern-day source on Satanism that I could find with the goal of not only assessing the world's perception of Satanism, but what I believed I could contribute to improve upon it. In this endeavor, not only did I find that traditionalism was, essentially, extinct, but that much of the world held a *horribly*

disfigured, asinine, and twisted view of traditional Satanism – not just Christians and the god-fearing, but many practitioners of the Left-Hand Path, too.

After this initial foray into modern Satanism, I was left with a sickening feeling of disappointment and shame – this was **not** the noble, Herculean religion that I had come to respect and, at one point, that I reviled as an aspirant priest. What I was looking at was a ghost of something greater – an *abominable* mockery of a faith that once demanded admiration, yet now clung desperately to the forgotten vestiges of its former glory – withered, gaunt, and soulless.

During my clerical studies, I read countless books on Satanic worship – many of which were written between the 14th and 19th centuries and bore little-to-no resemblance to what I saw lining the shelves of today's bookstores and occult gift shops – most of these New Age books offered a *palpable* lack of passion, integrity, and honesty that I could taste in every word, line, and page that I digested – I knew, without a doubt, that I *had* to address this problem.

In light of my grim discovery, I decided to accept the responsibility of giving Satanism a voice that I felt it deserved – I would become a mouthpiece of Hell on Earth, restoring honor, power, and dignity to the whole of Satanism by teaching the old-world ways of our religion to those willing to learn – to witches, Satanists, professors, critics, and even the Christians – to *anyone* willing to consider our side of the story, forgotten to and loathed by the world.

Therein, I began to hone my ability as a writer with the hope of resurrecting theistic Satanism from the archives of the ancient world – in this endeavor, I believe that I succeeded when I wrote *The Infernal Gospel* and offered it to the Left-Hand Path. With *The Infernal Gospel*, thousands of people learned about theistic Satanism for the first time, and their judgments were forever altered as they realized the true nature of traditional Satanism – a religion that inspires justice, knowledge, strength, honorability, and self-governance – it was **not** the cruel, *hateful* religion that the world has lamented for centuries.

No more evident were these characteristics than in the Infernal Tenets – and, in the days following the release of *The Infernal Gospel*, I watched with awe as something unfolded before my eyes like a fever dream – the unified praise for and implementation of these Infernal Tenets by atheistic and traditional Satanists alike, for they had clearly felt the honesty and genuine intentions of my words. Despite being a traditional Satanic minister, practitioners of *both* paths began to embody and spread the five Infernal Tenets like a *wildfire* – like a diabolical inferno of the most spectacular and awe-inspiring magnitude.

The point of this backstory is twofold – foremost, by knowing the events and motivations that led me to write *The Satanic Philosopher*, I hope to build a degree of trust and rapport with my readers – that would be *you.* As well, I have written *The Satanic Philosopher* in a way that is structured around the five Infernal Tenets, since they are the parameters by which I believe traditional Satanism should be followed for optimal growth and success – bearing this in mind, I felt that it was apropos (or, *at least* interesting,) to share the history behind the events, motivations, and beliefs that led to their formation.

I have sectioned *The Satanic Philosopher* into five core chapters, each discussing in detail one of the five Infernal Tenets – you will come to know these tenets as *Devotion*, *Resilience*, *Clarity*, *Autonomy*, and *Wisdom* – they are, together, what I believe it means to embody the old-world ways of Satanism and to be a traditional Satanist. These tenets, when *fully* applied to one's life, should be able to reforge even the most crestfallen soul into an unbreakable, honorable, and illustrious beacon of Hell on Earth.

THE FIRST TENET

CALLED

DEVOTION

Our first tenet is Devotion, and it is the cornerstone of traditional Satanism – without it, the Satanist is destined for disappointment, both in life and upon the Left-Hand Path. There exists nothing beautiful, extravagant, inspiring, or enlightening that may be attained without being devoted to its fruition – the most nectarous fruits of life shall be tasted **only** by those willing to sacrifice their time, energy, effort, patience, and perhaps even a portion of their sanity to caretaking whatever it is they wish to bear fruit.

How else does one taste the autumn apple, witness the building of a monument – or write a book? Any achievement, prize, or triumph of significant value requires a significant investment – **nothing** in this life will come to those that put forth minimal effort and expect a substantial result – power only comes to those that work for it, and are willing to sacrifice

55

whatever is necessary in order to reach their goals, aspirations, and the growth that they judge worthy of pursuing with what little time we have on Earth.

In this chapter, I will discuss the ways in which the tenet of Devotion reflects the fervor and passionate nature of traditional Satanism – as well, I shall *also* explore the ways in which you may apply this tenet in your everyday life and upon the Left-Hand Path. I believe that this Infernal Tenet, if *fully* embraced, shall inspire you to walk the road that leads to the gates of Hell – the Satanist that applies the Infernal Tenet of Devotion to their ember-paved path shall, in time, dine upon the bounties of our Lord Satan.

THE BEAST WITHIN

There is a beast within you – it hungers, and howls, and whispers to your errant soul in ancient tongues of devilment. This beast is born of your clay – it is an extension of your earthly being and your spirit's ether, wrapped in hellfire and the shadow of Satan.

It is your duty to nurture this beast – to caretake it, and bring order to its wild nature. It is a bridge that, if tended to, tamed, and followed, shall lead you to the gates of Hell – there, wherethrough the faithful may roam and behold the sybaritic fruits of Satan's kingdom – the sights, sounds, and many pleasures offered to *every* apostle that dares to take his mark.

This notion – *the beast* – what is it, and where does it come from? It is a vague and ambiguous term at best, yet for *millennia* it has enchanted every mind around the world with visions of devils, sacrilege, and unrepentant blasphemy – it conjures within all that walk this Earth the image of a horned dissenter of God – to most people, when they hear the term "the beast," they think of our savior – Lord Satan.

While this pairing seems to make obvious sense at first glance, its etymology is *actually* based on the misinterpretation of numerous verses found within the infamous Book of Revelation. Satan is referred to as many things throughout the Holy Bible – the adversary, deceiver, dragon, serpent – but he is not once referred to as the beast. The verses that many people for centuries have misinterpreted speak not of Satan, but of an Antichrist and the False Prophet of the end times – yes, **an** Antichrist. Many people are unaware of it, but the Bible alludes to *multiple* Antichrists – a multitude of people who have taken the mark of Hell, and who shall spread the word of our Lord Satan in the days leading up to his advent.

In today's world, though it is an ancient invention born from misunderstood scripture, we *continue* to refer to Satan as the beast – not just in Christianity and Catholicism, but in Satanism, as well. Though many Satanists are aware of this term's inaccurate origins, we choose to continue utilizing it as a term of endearment – when not spoken in a derogatory tongue, this term serves as another means for the worshipful disciple to acknowledge and celebrate the defiant, cunning, and *powerful* nature of Satan.

As well as referring to Satan, "the beast" is used in the modern-day by occultists to reference the beast within – but what is *this* beast? Well, the answer is complex and malleable, for it is determined by the unique values and beliefs of every Satanist – it is a psychological metaphor to some practitioners, and to others, it denotes the *literal* essence of Hell that we have allowed to reshape our unhallowed souls.

I believe that the beast within denotes the spirit of the Satanist – it is the culmination of every dream, ambition, appetite, passion, and pleasure that you hold dear as both a human being and an apostle of our Lord Satan. This beast within you *is* you – it is the deepest part of your being that shall guide you to power, pleasure, and wonder – it is the polestar of decadence that, if followed, shall lead you to the fruits of Hell, the bounties of Earth, and all that lies between these two kingdoms of guiltless pleasure.

In traditional Satanism, we believe that one's inner beast is sacred and inviolable – it is an ancient part of the Satanist's psyche that *must* be embraced, if one desires the mark and bounties of our kingdom of Hell. Only those that have welcomed their inner beast shall receive this infernal mark, for they have exemplified the spirit of Satan – courageous, wise, unyielding, and willing to denounce the path of the many in exchange for the strength and knowledge wielded by the few – by those that dared to rebuke the light and embrace the freedom of the darkness.

As you consider my point, I urge you to reflect on the origins of Satan. In Heaven, Lucifer's seat was at the left-hand side of God's throne. Lucifer's title came with *every* PG-13 pleasure, honor, accolade, and liberty that Heaven would allow – yet this was *far* from being satisfactory, or fulfilling. The beast within Lucifer – his *unfulfilled* nature, needs, and desires as an independent spirit – would eventually consume him, leading to his infamous insurrection and, ultimately, his damnation as he and his angels set siege to the pious, tyrannical kingdom of God.

Before Lucifer was cast out from Heaven, he was stripped of *everything* – his name, title, status, and his seat at the left-hand side of God. Then, he was given a new name – Satan, the adversary. He, *then*, was cast out from Heaven alongside those that had supported his rebellion. And they fell – plunging, twisting, and burning like meteors as they spiraled from that seraphical kingdom that we call Heaven.

As Satan and his angels plunged deeper and deeper into that black pit of penance, and uncertainty – the failed prison of God that would be rebuilt into our glorious kingdom of Hell – they *celebrated*. Their laughter pierced through the cindered smog and air with every laborious breath they managed to steal, as they plummeted through all of creation – Satan and his angels rejoiced, for the long-shackled and beaten beasts within them had *finally* been set free.

Though grave were the costs of his defiance, Satan believed that no cost was greater for one to suffer than the condemnation of one's nature, autonomy, dreams, and desires – *the beast within*. Though his seat in Heaven offered glory, applause, and safety, the cost was *far* too great – Satan was commanded to repress his ambitions, pleasures, and dreams of achievement. God described these desires as pride, yet Satan *insisted* that they were his right as a free and intelligent being – and, *too*, that human beings deserved the *same* liberties that God was decrying.

It was this disagreement over God's condemnation of free will and self-governance that instigated the conflict that I refer to as "The Grand Revolt." Had Lucifer continued to smother the beast within him for the sake of preventing discomfort and ridicule, not only would he and his angels *continue* to serve a tyrant at the cost of their liberty, but humankind would continue to flounder as just another aimless, thoughtless, and unremarkable animal upon Earth.

There are many lessons to be taken from the story of Lucifer's rebellion – foremost, that **nothing** is more precious and vital than one's freedom. There exists no creature on Earth or beyond that does not deserve the basic right to govern themselves in a virtuous and dignified fashion without the threat of violence by a higher, despotic power. As well, the tale of Lucifer's rebellion speaks to the importance of believing in oneself, no matter the obstacles that stand before you. It is within the power of each and every Satanist to endure the difficulties associated with the pursuit of self-betterment – to choose the path not of least resistance, but of optimal growth, regardless of whether or not that path is paved with uncertainty, fear, mockery, or condemnation by all the world and those that wish to see you surrender.

In traditional Satanism, we believe that one's inner beast is representative of their unrealized potential as both a human being and an apostle of Satan. By embracing the beast within, the Satanist pledges to act in harmony with their nature as a wise, rational, autonomous, and industrious being – someone that shall *always* aim to better themselves, never giving in to the cruelties of life or choosing the easy path.

If the Satanist does not act in a way that is true to their nature, I believe that disaster is only a matter of time – look at the story of the fall of Lucifer, as evidence to that notion. Our Lord Satan was forced to repress and refuse his nature under the threat of expulsion, derision, torment, and damnation – and what happened? His nature – the shackled, *beaten* beast within him – it eventually broke free from its prison, causing untold chaos in his life and setting in motion a ripple effect of *disastrous* proportions that echoed through the eons up until this very day.

When a person denies who they *really* are and the things that matter most to them, it is only a matter of time before the façade shatters and unleashes an errant, subjugated soul. I believe it is best to avoid self-deception altogether by searching inward and rejoicing in one's infernal nature – embracing the beast within and embracing one's potential as both a human being and as a disciple of our Lord Satan.

A LESSON FROM ICARUS

As Lucifer was stripped of his status and authority in Heaven, God would accuse Lucifer of being too proud, and too passionate – like Icarus, blinded by excitement and his desire to feel the molten kiss of the Sun, ultimately leading to his untimely demise.

While pride and passion are rarely considered bad or destructive traits, there *is* a morsel of truth in the aforesaid accusation. Though they are regarded as the traits of the most powerful people to have ever walked this Earth, pride and passion have *also* led to the downfall of just as many people. If a person is too proud or too passionate in their pursuits, they run the risk of flying too close to the Sun – just like our friend Icarus, the enraptured escapee of Crete.

While I believe Lucifer was justified in his defiant uprising against God's edicts, both Satan and God are no strangers to overindulging in passion – and it is seldom for the better. Perhaps it is the fate of those with absolute power to eventually abuse and bastardize their authority? Well, it is possible, but *improbable* – I believe what is more likely the case is that your average person is unfit to wield power of any sizeable caliber. Your average person with power is like a squid with a machinegun – they are likely to, at *some* point, use that power in a terrible, lamentable way. The vast majority of people that possess absolute power will become cruel, corrupt, unstable, dishonest, and *dangerous* – if you desire evidence for my assertion, open a history book and look to just about any figure that wielded absolute power – how few of them did not *eventually* create Hell on Earth for the people that they could reach.

Absolute power does not corrupt – *people* corrupt, and so, *too*, do the weaknesses, moral failures, and illusions that make them irresponsible with power. If you look back at any historical figure led astray by the thirst for and misuse of absolute power, you will find many traits in common: recklessness and impulsivity, a damaged ego that *somehow* coexists with a superiority complex, and a malleable moral compass. You see, the misuse and abuse of power is not the fault of power – just like the misuse of a firearm is not the fault of the firearm. I believe that *people* are the problem – weak, selfish, delusional, morally bankrupt people with their small emotions and unresolved instabilities. It is a *glorious* burden to walk through life with a significant measure of power at arm's length, and it should be treated like the gift that it is – a tool that allows you to change the world, help people, and create for yourself the idyllic life that you have *always* dreamt of leading.

What a person does with their opportunities, goals, difficulties, and power will determine their life and the stroke of their fortune. It is not passion or pride that leads to ruin, but rather, the factors that led to pride and passion in the first place – the motives, nature, impulses, repression, and desires of a given person. It is, therefore, within the ability of every Satanist to *healthily* revel in pride and pursue their every dream with passion – all while avoiding the fate of Icarus, of Nero, of Nebuchadnezzar, and all others that have lost themselves in passion's mire.

It is well-known that pride and passion are a staple of Satanic principles, and that is *especially* true for traditional Satanism. In fact, it is *because* our faith promotes these values that I speak so unyieldingly about the importance of behaving in a disciplined, rational, clear-headed, and honorable manner at *all* times, as you walk the ember-paved road that leads to Hell. You must exemplify composure, decency, and nobility, so that you may avoid the lachrymose fate of the *myriad* Satanists that have fallen before you – those that have sunken to the ruinous depths of corruption, sorrow, and regret, all because they abused the power that they attained in their studies upon their Left-Hand Path of traditional Satanism.

As I stated earlier in *The Satanic Philosopher*, it is **our** duty as traditional Satanists to focus not only on how we may attain power, but how we may do so without senselessly damaging ourselves, others, or the integrity of our religion. There is no nobility in stepping on others or destroying one's life in the pursuit of power – true strength is **not** amassed on the backs of the weak, but, rather, on the shoulders of the strong and those that are eager to serve as an example of what it means to be worthy of power.

There is a way to ascend *unimaginable* summits of power both within Satanism and in life itself – it is through generosity, honorability, and an eagerness to uplift and inspire others that you will, *ironically*, see the greatest benefit for yourself – even the tale of Lucifer's rebellion is testament to this truth. The miser that locks away their riches of wisdom from others shall surely protect said wisdom – but it will come at the cost of the opportunities that become available once a person decides to guide, motivate, and empower others. The Satanist that exemplifies the worthiness to wield power will become a force of change and positive enlightenment in the world, and this shall benefit *everyone* – the lives of other people will be invigorated through the presence of the Satanist, and the Satanist will more easily reap whatever pleasures they seek from this mortal life.

Above all, we encourage the traditional Satanist to embrace the beast within – to assess *every* desire, dream, pleasure, vice, and passion that is crucial to them and determine to what extent they are willing to go to satiate these needs. If you learned anything from my prior examples, it should be that passion is a wonderful trait to have – but if it does not have boundaries or limitations, it can quickly become a source of suffering, ruination, and self-damnation. By assessing what it is you want from life and the Left-Hand Path and determining what lengths you are willing to go to for their attainment, you reduce the likelihood that you will push the boundaries of your pursuits into treacherous territories. I believe that this is one of the best preventive measures for *anyone* that plans to embark on a pursuit of power.

The Satanist that recognizes and keeps in mind the significance of self-restraint shall always excel *far* beyond the Satanist that is unwilling to tame their reckless ways. Oftentimes, the Satanists that mock and deride the idea of self-limitation are those that walk a barren path of cataclysms – they become an Ouroboros of self-destruction as their impassioned ways breed chaos that further fuels and encourages their juvenile, unmanageable, and primitive paths.

Like Icarus, the Satanist that floods their heart with unbridled passion **will** meet an unpleasant fate – if caution is not taken as to what, how, and why one pursues what they pursue, a simple flight towards sanctuary might very well lead into the Sun. If you desire proof as to how quickly and cruelly passion might drag one to the Earth, take a quiet look at the world around you – at its silent atrophy, at the litter of failed dreams that fill the alleyways, and at the self-imposed desecration that paints the Earth with melancholia – *this* is the work of unrestrained ego, desire, wickedness, and excess on full display, all of which is the byproduct of passion and those that lived beyond the necessary confines of discipline. It is within your power to avoid this gruesome fate that has claimed so many promising souls – in your hands and in your heart, you have *every* necessary tool to triumph over the odds of failure. Do not let your current self and your future potential fall prey to the treacherous-yet-tempting powers of passion.

If you have assessed your desires, welcomed your inner beast, and committed to the Left-Hand Path of traditional Satanism – what else is barring your ember-scorched road to infernal godhood? Why is it that you are not where you wish to be, and where else would you have preferred to be by now? Well, whatever your answer is – plot your course and be on your way, because your decisive action is the *only* means by which you shall fulfill your dreams.

A KINGDOM OF ONE

The tenet of Devotion is twofold in nature – there is, foremost, the message of being devoted to one's innermost needs and psychology, but there is *also* the message of being devoted to the externals that offer additional value to the Satanist – the people, events, and causes that fill their heart with hellfire.

There is no refuting that Satanism, historically, has *always* been a religion that promoted solitude and selfishness – and there is nothing inherently wrong with that message. The psychology behind having this attitude *does* make sense – you should be your greatest priority in life, because you cannot help or contribute to others in any meaningful sense if you cannot, first, help and caretake your own needs. It is a reflection of the old saying, "you cannot pour from an empty cup" – which I believe is very true.

However, I believe the mistake of many Satanists is that they take this approach to life and faith with a sense of permanence – and *this* must change. The world is not meant to be divided, and there is little pride in hermitude for the sake of living up to some false idea of what it means to be a "true" Satanist.

It does not require strength to be selfish, and if any person would disregard or sacrifice others for their own gain, I would deem that person a coward. The world is *full* of people stepping on their neighbors in order to get a centimeter ahead in the grey, drab, and self-aggrandizing circus that we boldly regard as the modern, civilized world. It is a horror show.

There *is* a place for selfishness in Satanism, and in all other avenues upon the Left-Hand Path – but it should not be viewed as the permanent solution to dealing with one's problems. You have *every* right to be your top priority, but you have no right to act as if the rest of the world is expendable, or that the person next to you should disregard their priorities and cater to your sense of self-importance. I have had the misfortune of meeting many Satanists that thought and behaved in such a way, and their path, in the end, became a spectacle of self-annihilation.

It is not uncommon for the occultist to walk a quiet and lonely path, either *by* or *against* their will. The

Left-Hand Path is a commitment that not everyone understands – in fact, millions of people are deeply *terrified* of those that study the occult – especially us blasphemous souls that *dare* worship the Devil.

You must realize that we, as occultists, do not view the Left-Hand Path in the same light that much of the world does. Where others see uncertainty, evil, and repulsion, we see mystery, knowledge, and an unconscious need to understand the long-forgotten secrets of the immaterial world. Where others feel discomfort and distrust, we feel *excitement*, for we have witnessed arcane truths that have been hidden for *centuries*, if not longer. Where you and I see an opportunity for power, the rest of the world sees a disaster waiting to unfold – though it never comes.

The overwhelming majority of non-occultists are fearful of what they do not understand – and many of them do not care to learn. You and I, however – we have something within us that is awakened and inspired by the idea of discovery – of being one of a few that have looked upon some powerful, secret knowledge from our ancient past or from a strange world beyond our own. It is an exhilarating feeling that *cannot* be accurately conveyed to a person that has not felt and experienced it for themselves – and it is because of this, foremost, that many occultists walk the path of least resistance – that of solitude.

There is a preciousness to solitude that should not be undervalued – especially in the 21st century, the world appears to have forgotten the fruits of power and beauty that might be tasted when one's path is not burdened by the masses. The uninterrupted and uninfluenced thought; the purposefulness of one's ambitions; the ability to focus, without distraction, on the illumination of one's mind, flesh, and spirit – *these* are the blessings that solitude may provide.

However, these blessings are only seen as such by those that have *willingly* chosen solitude – to those that have been cast out into the darkness without a light, these blessings are curses. The uninterrupted thought becomes a cesspit of misery, and pain; the freedom to choose one's path becomes paralyzing; the idea of sitting with oneself and assessing what, why, and how they wish to alter their life becomes as terrifying to them as it is comforting for you or me – the gift of solitude is only seen as such if the person in question has chosen to embrace its path.

On the Left-Hand Path, I believe solitude is, often, one of your greatest allies. As an occultist, you will enjoy your most *extraordinary* moments of growth when nobody is around to witness you – in the late morning hours, when all the world is sleeping and dreaming of magical things; during your very first rituals, as you introduce yourself to the spirits of a faraway world; under midnight's icy moon; in the woodlands, over the barrows, and in the forgotten corners of the Earth where only spirits still reside, you shall find yourself alone, more often than not.

As beauty may be found in solitude, so, *too*, may it be found in the unification of those that live and pray as one. The power that thunders in the united voice of Satan's celebrants is the song that echoes throughout the halls, hollows, and ember-wrought shadows of our kingdom of Hell. It is the sound of devils and apostles rejoicing as one under the reign of our Lord Satan – unified, defiant, and proud to feast upon the bounties of Hell beside their fellow kinsmen – beside those that bear the infernal mark of beasts, and who have blessed their mortal souls in the Promethean flames of our kingdom of Hell.

As a traditional Satanist, there are few experiences that will surpass the vigor that shall fill your heart, once you stand amongst your kin – amongst those that have peered into the fires of Hell and seen the reflection of their bestial soul. To be amongst your kinsmen – *even* if only in spirit, or thought – there are few feelings in the world that rival its potency.

And, like Lucifer and his wayward angels as they plummeted from Heaven, you will celebrate – you will rejoice amongst your kin – amongst those, like you, who have proudly accepted the cindered mark of Satan. Your laughter will carve through the air, and you will crash through the Earth like primeval lightning destined for the gates of Hell – and there, I will join you – and we will revel in Satan's grace.

There is always a tremendous price that one must pay for *true*, transcendental power – unfortunately, we rarely know what those costs are until after the fact, when Fate appears with her tin cup rattling in search of alms. It is an uncomfortable reality of the life of an occultist, but *especially* for a person that has pledged their soul to Satan and our kingdom of Hell – for us, there always appears to be an unusual price to pay for the diabolical blessings we receive.

This is where the decriers of Satan will claim that we are being punished, or deceived by the Devil's malevolent ways – that if we were to worship God instead of Satan, there would be no price to pay for our salvation. I disagree, and I will make a counter argument – the price to pay for fealty to a tyrant is *far* worse than the cost of siding with a misjudged god that has your best interest at heart – a god that was eternally damned for defending **you** when you did not have the voice or ability to defend yourself.

The reality of the matter is that no Satanist has *ever* suffered due to their faith itself – the suffering that Satanists endure is either self-inflicted, or it is the result of prejudice and cruelty in a fearful world. I believe that people are to blame for **every** form of suffering that exists – to push the guilt of our own actions onto the shoulders of gods, monsters, stars, Satan, or anything else divine is little more than an attempt to downplay the barbarism and hatefulness of the human race. So, let us be clear on one thing, above all else – neither God nor Satan are to blame for how poorly we treat one another. It is the work of people and people alone for the *horrific* state we now find the world in – Satan is merely a spectator.

It is critical that the Satanist carefully considers the path they travel, and how they wish to continue on its course – that they are making the right choices, for the right reasons. If one prefers solitude, then I encourage it – but do you honestly *prefer* isolation, or is it just something that you became accustomed to? And, for the extraverted Satanist – do you truly enjoy being lost amongst the crowd, or are you too afraid of finding out who you really are, when you are left alone with the infinite chaos of your mind?

As you can see, what might initially appear to be a preference might *actually* be one's conditioning to circumstances that they otherwise would not have chosen – and, since you are now in control of your path, **you** have the ability to make a choice that is different than the one you originally had no say in.

It is up to the discretion of each individual Satanist to determine what will work best for them – in life, their studies, and everything in between. My word is not law, but it *is* caring advice from an old soul that has dealt with his fair share of self-reflection, regret, misjudgment, and miscalculation about life itself, and how best to prosper amidst its darkness.

YOUR CRUCIFIXION

If you have welcomed the beast within you, and if you have made peace with the potential drawbacks that come with the life and path of a Satanist, only one question remains – how far are you willing to go, in exchange for a fruitful and *remarkable* life?

If the Devil stood before you with your dreams and desires in the palm of his hand, what would you be willing to trade for their manifestation? And, if he were to inform you that you must, first, weather an unfair tempest of suffering *before* you could taste the fruits of your idyllic life – would you still be willing to make a deal with the Devil? Would you still believe that your idea of a perfect life is worth pursuing if you *knew* that your pain was vital to its fruition? This is the question that you must answer.

The reason that I present this question to you is not to suggest that Satan is out to get you – though the world would love for you to believe that the Devil is your archnemesis, determined to carry out your swift and *terrible* ruin – that is simply not the case.

As I stated in the prior subchapter, the suffering of the Satanist is either self-inflicted or inflicted upon one by the pious hand of another human being. It is, unfortunately, commonplace for outsiders to be roused by a sense of crusaderism once they realize that a Satanist is walking amongst them. Once our beliefs have been revealed to the masses, we, then, risk inheriting the fate of all other persecuted and reviled peoples – becoming a target for the cruelty and malevolence of those that *refuse* to accept that a person can live and pray differently than they do.

The collective ignorance of other people is a truly dangerous beast – an ignorant individual might be malevolent or dangerous, but, oftentimes, they are little more than an annoyance. The ignorant group, however, is *exceptionally* dangerous – especially when that group is motivated by hatred, fear, or the desire to triumph over a person, group, or ideology that they believe is an obstacle to or blasphemation of their religion, politics, comforts, or way of life. That said, while Satanism *does* evoke vitriolic and unpleasant reactions from many people, it seldom

84

devolves into a violent or physical reaction – harsh and derogatory words are more common than the credible threat of being burned at the stake. While your experiences will differ from mine, if it offers any solace – I have introduced myself as a Satanic minister to *countless* Catholics and Christians over the past decade, and only twice did it put me under the immediate threat of physical peril. It is usually the case that my status as a minister of Hell serves as a conversational point, even amongst those that follow the word of God – I am viewed as a sort of walking gaff, or an abomination so interesting that they cannot help but to get close and ask questions.

I find it disturbing that, in the 21st century, we must prepare ourselves for the possibility of falling prey to a witch-hunt – but that is the world that we live in. We must become comfortable with the idea of being persecuted for our beliefs, even if we are not harming anyone in the process. All that matters in the mind of the god-fearing crowd is that someone has *dared* to denounce the tyrannical word of God in favor of the Devil – it is a realization that many lambs of God seem to regard as a *challenge*, in my experience: "Perhaps if I cram enough Corinthians verses down their throat, it will force the Devil out of them?"– that is the broken thought process that I imagine goes through the mind of your everyday zealot of God, when they learn that your wretched, withered soul has *already* been sworn to the Devil.

I know that I am coming across more cynical than usual, at the moment – forgive us our trespasses. It is not my intention to scare you off from becoming a traditional Satanist, nor is it my intention to paint the world as your adversary. At the end of the day, it is my responsibility to provide you with *realistic* expectations of traditional Satanism and the things that you should anticipate if you decide to walk its path – and this includes any *potential* discomforts.

In general, the odds are *tremendously* low that you will run into any serious, perilous, or life-changing problems due *solely* to being a traditional Satanist. In most instances that a Satanist suffers significant retaliation for their beliefs, there is usually *another* factor involved that escalates the situation at hand into a violent confrontation – mocking, debating, criticizing, or threatening others, for example – not *always*, but I would say more often than not. What is more likely to happen is that you will experience periods of solitude, either imposed by others in an effort to distance themselves from the lowly devil worshipper, or by *your* own hand, in an attempt to distance yourself from the vitriol and theatrics of a world that so heartlessly enforces the word of God.

Though I believe it is improbable that you will find yourself at *serious* risk due to your religion, make no mistake – you **will** experience *some* measure of loss, pain, suffering, solitude, or discomfort that is a *direct* response to your faith from the rest of the uncivilized world. There will be pious comments, threats of violence, degradation, unwanted biblical scriptures, and invitations to church masses – there will be Catholics that vilify you, and ones that like you as a person, *despite* your beliefs – you will be alienated and viewed as a pariah, by some, and by others, you will be embraced with unbigoted arms.

The question is not a matter of *if* you will be faced with condemnation and suffering – it is a matter of whether or not you are willing to weather suffering in order to reach greatness – if you are prepared to

87

face the worst of people, the world, and life, as you stand firmly by your faith as a traditional Satanist.

The road to our kingdom of Hell is littered with the fruits of both power and sacrifice, and the Satanist *cannot* consume one without the other – if you are to cultivate and feast upon the bounties offered by our faith of traditional Satanism, then you must be prepared to pay a debt – a debt not issued by Satan, but by the rest of the world. The price of admission to our kingdom of Hell differs for *every* celebrant that walks through its ebon gates – it may be time, energy, money, or comfort. It might be solitude, or derision, or a difficult circumstance that forces you to reflect on your faults and weaknesses. You may lose friends, your family may reject you, and your community may label you a pariah. It is *impossible* to know exactly what price you will have to pay to follow your faith as a traditional Satanist, but find solace in the fact that, when the time comes, it will be up to you to either refuse or accept the payment.

It is your ability to *choose* if, when, why, and how you accept the cost of your pursuits that separates

sacrifice from **martyrdom** – you are not a martyr, you are a Satanist. It *will* require sacrifice to reach any meaningful distance on the Left-Hand Path of theistic Satanism, but these sacrifices will be *yours* to either accept or refuse – nobody will coerce you into pursuing your ambitions. Only you can decide the limits of the sacrifices that you are prepared to make in the pursuit of your idyllic life – it is up to you to decide if you can accept the sacrifices that arise, when it is time to make a deal with the Devil.

THE SECOND TENET

CALLED

RESILIENCE

Our second tenet is *Resilience* – the ability, nerve, and will of the Satanist to weather and conquer the trials and tribulations of life. This tenet denotes the importance of being able to withstand the cruelties and challenges that every Satanist *must* overcome, if they are to create for themselves their idyllic life.

If the Satanist wishes to feast upon the fruits of our kingdom of Hell – to revel in the bounties that all mortals dream of, yet few ever taste – they *must* be prepared to face and endure the dreadful tempests of life. Only those that are willing to walk through darkness will ever reach the light – it is the bravest of practitioners that attain the greatest of treasures.

Every *extraordinary* deed – every victory, success, and achievement – has been won by those that are bold of heart and unwavering in spirit. Only those that are willing to face and weather the cruelties of life will ever reap the gold within her cyclonic eye.

In this chapter, I will discuss the myriad ways that the tenet of Resilience reflects the fearless, valiant, and *courageous* nature of traditional Satanism. As I do so, I shall explore the philosophy of this tenet, as well as how it may be applied both in everyday life and upon the Left-Hand Path. If the Satanist is *truly* devoted to their faith, I believe that the tenet of Resilience will offer an *irreplaceable* feeling of self-reliance, strength, and the hardening of one's character in all ways necessary to attaining power.

LIKE THE CITY OF DIS

Above all else, I would regard the theistic Satanist as a symbol of power – a beacon of Hell on Earth, unbroken and undeterred by the wickedness of life and of those souls that would dare to trespass upon the Satanist's Left-Hand Path – the lambs of God, the detractors of the Devil, and those whose hearts beat to the war drums cruelty, fear, and ignorance. The theistic Satanist is unyielding – not by chance, but by *creation* – they have witnessed the strength and indomitability of Satan's philosophy, and they have chosen to embody it – to become as powerful, determined, and unconquerable as our Lord Satan.

How many times have you been beaten down and broken by life, without warning or reprieve? How many people do you know that exist in a *perpetual* state of suffering, turmoil, pain, and sorrow? There is a hideousness to life that cannot be denied – an unacknowledged specter of misery lurking around every corridor, within every home, between every headline, and in every heart – an inescapable ghost of tragedy that haunts every corner of the world we live in, possessing the wistful minds of humankind with a strangulating, *dispiriting* sensation of dread.

It is an ugly truth that cannot be avoided – so how does one live a good and fruitful life, amidst such hopeless circumstances? Well, by turning inwards and strengthening oneself – by becoming stronger, braver, and more resilient than the nightmares and terrors of the world. It *is* possible to live a beautiful life, despite the atrocities that surround us – but it requires the Satanist to look within themselves for the ability to transform, and become *powerful* – to become as steadfast as the walls and ramparts that shape and encircle the ember-scorched City of Dis.

If the Satanist cannot change the world, they must, then, improve themselves – they must adapt to and prosper in spite of the circumstances that they have been crippled by, and this *demands* resilience. The pursuit of a better life is not easy – that is why most people would rather accept and make the best out of a terrible life – because it is far easier to stomach the bad than it is to fight for something better, and the majority of people are not interested in fighting for the opportunity to suffer. That is what pursuing your idyllic life *means*, at its core – to fight for the opportunity to suffer in exchange for sculpting the picturesque life that you truly believe you deserve.

As I discussed in the previous chapter, anything of extraordinary value entails extraordinary sacrifice. Life does not offer handouts – you will have to pay for every inch of ground that you claim for the life you wish to create for yourself. If you are resilient, determined, and able to endure the difficulties that this journey will pose, then it will make you all the more likely to succeed in your Herculean pursuits.

If the Satanist wishes to be resilient, they must first confront their inner disturbances – life's obstacles will prove *considerably* easier to deal with if one's mind is free from emotional wreckages, and this is accomplished through the pursuit of *self-mastery*. At the heart of traditional Satanism, you shall find the pursuit of self-mastery – the interminable goal of always remaining in control of one's emotional, mental, and spiritual soundness, while doing your best to *also* uphold the physical – since you cannot directly control the world, your body, or the things that happen to you, it takes backseat precedence to those parts of yourself that you can *always* control.

It is crucial for you to realize that, try as you might, the only thing in this world *completely* and *forever* under your control is **you** – how you think, behave, speak, and exist as a human being – anything else might be *affectable*, but is innately uncontrollable. The more time you waste trying to change, control, and alter everything around you *except* for you, the longer you will continue being less than you could be. As a traditional Satanist, you should be focused on controlling and altering yourself – whatever the world is doing around you is irrelevant, so long as you continue to be at the mercy of its happenings.

Ironically, those that attempt to control everything around them, in turn, end up *being* controlled – the person whose mental, emotional, or spiritual peace can be governed by the world, its difficulties, or its denizens is a slave – a soul conquered by triviality, weakness, discomfort, and an obsession to control every aspect of life *except* for themselves. It is one of the worst forms of subservience and bondage in the eyes of a traditional Satanist – the sacrifice and

96

tarnishing of one's inner potential in exchange for being preoccupied with a world that *despises* your existence. To allow oneself to be controlled by the clockworks of this pious world and its god-fearing masses is as close to a deviation from the values of traditional Satanism as would be worshiping God.

The Satanist that has mastered their own mind is a colossus – they cannot *ever* be conquered, for they have *already* conquered themselves. This is not an easy task, but it *is* a necessary one – if you wish to ever attain true power in life or upon the Left-Hand Path, you must be able to govern, guide, and direct yourself independently, without the interference of this rotten Earth and the mindless masses that plod its loam. The ability to live, prosper, and change in a way that is self-decided and uninfluenced by the world is, to me, a *true* demonstration of resilience.

To make yourself resilient is a difficult feat – to be able to calm your thoughts, subdue your emotions, and cultivate a sense of self-mastery will be one of the most difficult things that you ever do – if it was easy, the *entire* world and its inhabitants would be paragons of mental acuity, tolerance, compassion, and level-headedness. If the pursuit and attainment of self-mastery were a simple task, every aspect of life would change immeasurably in one fell swoop of utopian bliss – every war would grind to a halt; every conflict, dispute, and disagreement would be solved *instantaneously*; wickedness, fear, bigotry, egoism, and xenophobia would vanish in the blink of an eye – the Earth as we know it would cease to exist, for malice would become a distant memory.

I believe that self-mastery is the most difficult-yet-noble undertaking that a person can *ever* choose to embark on – it has no finish line, no accolades, and nobody to pick up the slack for you if you fall short of your ideals. It is just you and life, fighting it out until one of you surrenders – bloodied, beaten, and weak. With the philosophy of traditional Satanism, *however*, I believe that you have the *best* possible chances of victory – of conquering and prospering in spite of the many tempests of this terrible world that will try their very hardest to break your spirit.

It will not be immediate, and it will be *remarkably* challenging – but the only way that you shall ever cultivate resilience is by persisting in spite of and overcoming the *horrific*, unjust, brutal, and painful circumstances of life – the cruelties of this world, and the misfortunes that so plentifully bubble forth from its caliginous depths. As you do so, you must remember to keep close your faith – as a traditional Satanist, your faith is the light that shall guide you through the blackest of nights – the values, beliefs, principles, and philosophy of traditional Satanism will *always* be there for you, prepared to empower and inspire your triumph over the tempests of life.

That said, you might very well find that your faith *also* becomes one of the future challenges that will require your courage and resilience. As the outside world learns of your beliefs, it is possible that they will heap obstacles upon your path – and it will be up to you to decide the best course for handling it. If you wish to ever taste the fruits of our kingdom of Hell, then you must be able to withstand the fire along the way – you must be prepared and willing to stand boldly like the ember-wrought City of Dis.

WHERE NOBODY ELSE WILL GO

It is in our nature, you, and I, to explore the secrets and realms where others *dare* not venture – to look upon and taste the fruits of arcane knowledge from forgotten kingdoms and hidden worlds – it is in the nature of our inner beasts, to go where nobody else would *ever* go in pursuit of transcendental power.

We are willing to go to extents for self-betterment that most other people are **not** prepared to go – we understand how crucial it is to be strong, wise, and resilient in a world that devours the weak – a world that has lost its mind and soul to madness, cruelty, and a thirst for destroying *all* things judged outlier.

It is in these places and moments of solitude where the Satanist will often find themselves – in the old bibliotheca of a monastery; at the fiery altarside of an ancient demon; standing alone for an honorable and forthright cause; searching inwards, and fixing the scars that litter one's mind, flesh, and soul – in many instances that require courage, resilience, or devotion, the Satanist will oftentimes stand alone.

If you look around you at the events of the modern world, it is a common theme – a handful of people, standing as one against an overwhelming threat or *impossible* odds, whether it be a disease, an army, a sociopolitical uprising, or anything else – it is the courageous few that often stand against the many.

As a traditional Satanist, you *will* stand against the many – not as a courier of conflict, but as a person devoted to a religion that enrages the world. As an unyielding herald of Hell on Earth, you are bound to meet people who regard the mark of Satan as a target – a bullseye at which they may project their hatred, and derision, and opposition – an outlet for them to spit upon with the venom of their wretched souls. As a traditional Satanist, you will oftentimes stand alone – you will weather the tempests of life and the malice of the pious with *nothing* but your faith as a bulwark and your soul as your sanctuary.

I believe that there is a heroism to the Satanist – an oft-unacknowledged honor in one's willingness to defy the world in order to stand by the religion that brings them strength, peace, camaraderie, wisdom, resilience, and dignity. The cost for these blessings is not cheap, as you know – sacrifice, solitude, and the disdain of the world is no small price to pay for one's spiritual freedom. And yet, we are willing to pay this cost anyways, even if it means that we will be cast out into the night – perhaps that threat does not strike fear into the Satanist, though, for the fire of their soul will always light the way back home.

I am no stranger to a path of solitude. As of writing *The Satanic Philosopher*, I have spent a decade of my life serving as a Satanic minister – and *most* of those years have been spent alone. Oftentimes, this solitude has been by choice, but occasionally it has been due to circumstances beyond my control. The life of a religious leader is not exactly easy to share with others – friends, family, romantic partners. In the pursuit of my dream to heal and empower our faith of theistic Satanism, I have had to sacrifice a *substantial* portion of my life – *thousands* of hours that I will never reclaim; relationships forever lost; opportunities forsaken in favor of writing; mental, emotional, and physical exhaustion; scorn, cruelty, condemnation, and threats of violence – these are just a portion of the costs that I have had to pay, in exchange for the potential to manifest my dreams.

Though my sacrifices have been difficult, they are *far* easier for me to stomach than the idea of failing my potential, pissing away my dreams, and living an unremarkable life – and for what? So that I can sometimes enjoy the company of other people that have *also* squandered their potential? So that I can settle for the easy path that does not pose any scary challenges or uncertainties – because God forbid I have to improve myself as a human being, right? I **chose** my sacrifices *every* step of the way because I believe that the path of self-betterment is always nobler than the well-trodden path of no resistance.

I believe that sacrifice is *always* required, if one is to achieve anything worthwhile in life – remember when I stated that anything of extraordinary value requires extraordinary sacrifice? Well, I am a great example of that assertion's truth – if I did not make the sacrifices I have and continue to make, there would be no "Rev. Cain." *The Infernal Gospel*, *Ars Diabolica*, and now *The Satanic Philosopher* – the many books that I have tirelessly authored for the past decade would cease to exist and, therefore, the work that I have done to heal traditional Satanism would have never manifested. Everything that you know from my work would suddenly vanish, for it would be *forever* locked away within the annals of my mind – never to see the light of day or cross the eyes of another person, *all* because of fear and an unwillingness to experience a bit of discomfort.

Only you can decide your fate – your path, actions, sacrifices, and to what extent you are willing to go in the pursuit of your dreams. If you desire power, wealth, knowledge, or achievement – if you desire transcendental wisdom from the Left-Hand Path or the blessings of our Lord Satan – you must accept that these fruits will *not* come cheaply, nor without sacrifice. The master occultist attains their wisdom at the cost of time, as they toil away *thousands* of hours studying the knowledge of forgotten epochs. The miser that sits upon their mountain of gold has attained their riches at the cost of happiness, effort, or energy. The king that rules a castle has inherited his crown at the cost of violence, death, or the envy of those that covet his throne. The cost of all great achievements is expensive – but it is *also* up to the person in question, whether or not they are willing and able to make the sacrifices necessary to realize their hopes, dreams, desires, and worldly pursuits.

Though every person is entitled to a joyous life and basic human rights, **no** person is entitled to live an *extraordinary* life – the sweetest fruits should only be tasted by the people that are willing to suffer for their attainment – not because I believe that people deserve to suffer, but, rather, because I believe that effort, sacrifice, and resilience should be rewarded with the most precious treasures that life can offer.

So, the question remains – can you withstand what difficulties you will face upon the Left-Hand Path, in exchange for the blessings it may offer? Are you willing and prepared to endure the trials, torments, and tribulations that the world may wish to impose upon you – all because you dare to call yourself a theistic Satanist? Are you willing to venture where nobody else will go, in the pursuit of self-mastery, conquest, and power – to the edge of the civilized world; to the lonely, ember-paved paths of infernal grace; to the summits of wisdom, and to the depths of desolation; to the gates of our kingdom of Hell?

THE COLOSSEUM OF LIFE

On the Left-Hand Path of traditional Satanism, the faith that you carry is your sword and shield – your commitment to your beliefs is the light that illumes the darkling road ahead, and your resilience is the reliquary that safeguards your hellbound soul. You have within you *every* tool and measure needed to overcome the surprises, obstacles, and horrors that await you just off your charted path – there, where prowls the pious, and the cruel, and those that wish to encumber your journey to our kingdom of Hell.

For as long you walk this Left-Hand Path, you will walk in the eye of malevolence – you will journey through vales of condemnation and the shadows of uncertainty, *perpetually* fixed within the malicious gaze of those that hunger for your downfall. There is nothing that you can do to avoid this truth, aside for cultivating the strength, courage, and resilience necessary to endure the trespassers that lie in wait.

Let us not mistake acceptance for victimhood – the inevitable run-in with obstacles is an unescapable truth of not only the Left-Hand Path, but of life and the pursuit of *any* form of self-empowerment. You will not find a single person on Earth that has been so fortunate as not to have experienced cruelties or difficulties due to their beliefs, dreams, or pursuits.

Oftentimes, it is the oft-untraveled road that offers the most ambrosial fruits – the road overgrown and forgotten by the outside world. The paths that bear the most valuable treasures and nectarous fruits are the paths of heavy resistance – the paths lined with challenges, perils, sacrifices, and Herculean trials, conquerable **only** by the strongest travelers. Upon these shadow-swathed paths, you shall encounter all matter of atrocities that *must* be conquered – the long-overlooked monstrosities of your mind; the ugliness of the world, and the cruelty of those that inhabit it; the temptations of your weaknesses, and your subconscious desire for self-destruction – the difficulties that lie ahead will require true strength to conquer, but it *will* be worth it. On the other side of the obstacles you will face, the most precious of all treasures await you – coveted by all but reaped by the few – it is the opulent jewel of *self-mastery*.

There is no treasure in Hell or on Earth that is more worth fighting for than self-mastery – the ability to control oneself independent of any thought, event, emotion, person, or challenge that aims to impede the will of the Satanist. While part of the pursuit of self-mastery involves autonomy, the third Infernal Tenet, it *also* requires both devotion and resilience in order to successfully pursue its attainment. If the Satanist is lacking in their devotion to their path, it will lead to ruin – and, too, if the Satanist is unable to withstand the trials of life, they will, *inevitably*, surrender to the world's gauntlets before they ever have a chance to savor the fruits of their sacrifice.

The importance of the Satanist's resilience *cannot* be overemphasized – no matter the devotion of the Satanist, if they cannot triumph over the trials that arise on the path of a traditional Satanist, they shall never attain the power that they desire. It is simply not enough to be faithful and spiritually devoted to one's path – the Satanist must *also* be resilient, and capable of weathering the opposition of the world and its many acts of Machiavellianism. That said, despite how unforgiving this all might sound, the

Satanist is **not** expected to be superhuman. People are inherently fallible – our bones break; our souls become crestfallen; our hearts wax and wane their devilish flames – such is the nature of *every* mortal being that walks this Earth. No – you are not meant be superhuman, but you *are* expected to always do your best to conquer the obstacles that impede you.

The spirit of traditional Satanism is one of infernal resolve, willpower, and persistence – of an almost *supernatural* relentlessness, even when faced with the most daunting odds or adversities – note that I said willpower and persistence, not invincibility. It is the nature of the traditional Satanist to persevere in the face of adversity – always pushing through the trials at hand not because it will prove easy, but because it is *necessary* for one's growth. The path of meaningful opposition will *always* impart those that weather its tempests with greater strength and wisdom than those that travel a challengeless path.

As traditional Satanists, we are taught to handle all conflict with the *same* verve – with poise, stillness, rationality, perseverance, and determination to see the tempests at hand through to the end, so long as we have determined it is a worthwhile endeavor. If there is something to be attained by weathering the tempest in question that is more valuable than it is painful to attain, then it is *generally* regarded as an endeavor worth our blood, sweat, effort, and tears.

While the philosophy of traditional Satanism *does* highlight the usefulness of cultivating strength and resilience, it also clearly stresses the ways in which the Satanist should and should not respond to life's adversities – above all else, that violence, hostility, and barbarism should *never* be the initial response to an obstacle or conflict. It is **not** a demonstration of strength, to turn to violence in order to get one's way – it is the tactic of a coward to promptly throw a tantrum, threaten, and wound other people when things do not unfold according to one's plan. If the only tool in your arsenal is to cause pain and chaos when matters do not go to your liking, then you are guilty of and complicit in the tyranny of the world.

It is the response of the self-mastered and powerful mind, to respond to adversity with composure – to accept and address the *torturous* tempests that rage before oneself with the stillness, patience, intrigue,

111

and poise of our Lord Satan. You must understand that life is intrinsically volatile, unpredictable, and dangerous – and this shall prove *especially* true on your journey to our kingdom of Hell – the road to which is *littered* with obstacles, oppression, grief, torment, injustice, and tests of one's resolve. If one is to ever achieve the blessings they seek from life or the Left-Hand Path of traditional Satanism, they *must* be able to weather the tempests that lie ahead with composure, determination, willpower, and an ability to face the hardships that lead to greatness.

There is no way around it – you *will* have to fight for the life that you desire. In the colosseum of life, there are no victories that come freely, and without sacrifice. It will be a fight for *every* inch of ground that you take as you traverse the Left-Hand Path of traditional Satanism – this fight is not one of steel, flesh, and blood, but of resilience, courage, and the *unyielding* resilience required to make the descent to our kingdom of Hell. If you are truly committed to your faith as a traditional Satanist – to sculpting your vision of an idyllic life, cultivating the gift of self-mastery, and dining upon the fruits of success, pleasure, strength, clarity, and divinity – you *must* become resilient. This resilience will not be found in violence, wickedness, or chaos, but through the conquering of one's mind, the steeling of the beast within, and embracing the spirit of our Lord Satan.

WEATHER THE STORM

There exists an undertone of calamity, gloom, and melancholy that corrupts the once-verdant loam of Earth – it pervades *every* instance of life, no matter how colossal or microscopic. In every moment and creation there is an almost *imperceptible* flicker of suffering – in the wingless flies that writhe atop an unkept mantle; in the scorched fields of a warzone; in the cruelty, isolation, and grey disquiet that fills the alleyways of our cities; in the broken stones of forgotten churchyards, now reclaimed by nature's insatiable hunger. All around us tides a Stygian sea of *suffering* – an irrefutable and inescapable abyss, acknowledged by few and survived by even fewer.

The tides of this aphotic sea are all-reaching – they erode every corner of this world, and they entomb every living soul beneath their sarcophagal deeps. It is the sadistic fate of *every* mortal soul that walks the Earth, to weather this sea of suffering – to each confront our own unique and dreadful storms, and endure despite their cruelties. There is no escaping the suffering of the Earth – it is an intrinsic part of our mortality, and, I would argue, it is an important part of our ability to thrive in and adapt to horrific odds, brutal circumstances, and perilous obstacles.

Thankfully, there *is* a positive side to this gloomy, dispiriting narrative that I have built – your ability to *clearly* perceive and address the tempests of life, thanks to the cultivation of self-mastery. As I have detailed throughout *The Satanic Philosopher* thus far, in your employment of self-mastery, the world ceases to control you – its disasters, heartlessness, and relentless sorrows. While these will *always* be viewed as some of life's more unpleasant realities, they shall no longer control your life by corrupting your judgment and therefore dictating the ways in which you perceive the world and its happenings. The power of self-mastery *cannot* be overstated or exaggerated – it is an extraordinary tool that *every* person has the ability to cultivate with experience, willpower, wisdom, resilience, patience, and time.

It is in the mind's contextualization of the things it experiences where we shape our judgments, fears, desires, and our views about what constitutes good or bad – and, because your brain wishes to protect you against the threats and perils of the world, it is preconditioned to label *every* emotion, experience, and event that has ever caused you discomfort as a negative and frightening specter. If you wish to be less reactive to the difficulties that both life and the Left-Hand Path will present, you may achieve this by reframing the trials that appear as *opportunities* to cultivate and finetune your grip on self-mastery.

As you follow the cinder-scorched path of theistic Satanism, you are *destined* to encounter rubble and ruins that block your way – the obstacles, vestiges, and barricades erected by the world and those that would trespass against the apostles of Satan. There is no avoiding these gauntlets of pious deterrence, but you *can* learn how to endure and conquer them without falling prey to their demoralizing agendas.

The obstructions that you shall face may only slow or impede your descent if you allow them to – they are only as strong as your reaction to their presence and those that orchestrated their creation. Though it is easier said than done, the best reaction to the obstacles set before you is to look upon them not

117

with anger, intimidation, or fear, but with laughter and entertainment – with pity for those that would waste their time attempting to trespass against and obstruct the pursuits of a devoted apostle of Satan.

I believe that the average person sacrifices *far* too much of themselves, to their problems – when they are faced with a tempest that appears too grave and gruesome to conquer, they perceive themselves as being too weak to weather its onslaught. The irony of this being that once a person regards themselves as being too weak to deal with their problems, they surrender their strength to the tempests at hand and therein fulfill their self-augured inability to handle the storm. When we respond to the tempests of life with terror, dread, and hopelessness, or foresee our demise through the lens of victimhood, we inhibit our ability to persevere – we surrender our strength to the tempests that assail us, therein feeding them and allowing them to grow stronger from the fruits of our self-sacrifice. It is not an easy feat, to endure the calamities of life with calmness and poise – but it is a *necessary* ability to learn, for **this** is how the traditional Satanist is able to weather such terrible, oppressive, gut-wrenching, and *tyrannical* storms.

It has been carved into the stars like prophecy – we are **all** destined to experience our own inescapable storms of suffering – the grim surprises, tragedies, misfortunes, and obstacles of life are plentiful, and we are each promised our generous share. There is no means by which you may avoid the cataclysms of life, but it is within your ability to learn how to *always* persevere no matter how bad the storm – as a traditional Satanist, you may *always* survive and prosper in spite of the obstacles that lie ahead. **You** are the key to your own salvation – though you are fated to the trials and gauntlets of life, it is always within your power to choose how you will respond to these challenges – it is up to you to decide how you will weather and respond to the storms of life.

Every being has its breaking point – every human, angel, demon, and god will *eventually* succumb to the burdens heaped upon their shoulders. We each are tethered to an Atlas stone of suffering – to our own world of potential Heaven or Hell. It is up to the discretion of each person to determine for how much longer they are willing to hoist that debt of anguish, in exchange for the fruition of their every dream – for how long one is prepared to endure the cruel onslaught of life and to what extents they are willing to go in the pursuit of their heart's desires.

There is no finite answer – there is no rubric, rule, or guideline for how much adversity or sacrifice a person should be willing to endure in exchange for their desires. As a traditional Satanist, you are the **only** person in control of your life's course – there is no other person that can rightly etch in stone the ways in which you should prioritize and pursue the victories and conquests that you covet for yourself.

Upon the Left-Hand Path of theistic Satanism, you will encounter *countless* obstacles – as I described in previously in *The Satanic Philosopher*, there is no shortage of challenges in the life of a traditional Satanist. From derision, scorn, and condemnation, to violence, prejudice, and solitude – from atheists, Catholics, and self-aggrandizing Satanists to your friends, family, and neighbors – from your doubts, fears, and insecurities to your weaknesses, egoism, anger, or diminished faith – the trials and gauntlets that lie in wait upon your path are *eternal*, never to be permanently escaped, avoided, or extinguished.

120

For as long as you walk this Earth and traverse the Left-Hand Path of traditional Satanism, challenges will arise from the grime and shadows to test your resolve – to prod the beast within you and see what your soul is made of – glass, or hell-wrought iron. As a fellow apostle of Satan's godship, I **know** that you will endure – the world does not win whenever it provokes the proud celebrants of our kingdom of Hell, nor do the heralds of God triumph over those that bear the burning mark of beasts – that ancient mark of devils, and those devoted to Satan's reign.

THE THIRD TENET

CALLED

CLARITY

Our third tenet is *Clarity* – the ability to recognize, without personal bias or distortion, the *true* nature of oneself, one's path, and the outside world. With a clear perception of everything that transpires, the Satanist will better know how to orient themselves in life and upon their Left-Hand Path of devilment.

If the Satanist hopes to ascend any notable heights of power, wisdom, or achievement, they *must* have the ability to soundly assess the road ahead – to see the events, obstacles, and surprises of life without preference – without being blinded and misguided by one's own, fear, arrogance, cruelty, judgments, paranoia, or any other filter that corrupts the truth.

How can one expect to *ever* taste the fruits of Hell, if they cannot accurately chart the path towards its gates? If the Satanist would allow themselves to be guided off-course from the road to our kingdom of Hell, how can they expect to ever revel, feast, and celebrate amongst their kin – amongst the apostles of our Lord Satan? To follow the path that leads to the bounties of Hell, the Satanist must have clarity.

In this chapter, I will discuss the ways in which the tenet of Clarity reflects the willpower and presence of mind of traditional Satanism. As I do so, I shall *also* explore the ways in which you may apply this tenet in your everyday life and upon the Left-Hand Path. If the Satanist wishes to see themselves, their life, and the Left-Hand Path without being blinded by self-deception, I believe that the tenet of Clarity shall offer them the guidance and sight they desire.

THE MIRROR'S JUDGMENT

What is it that you see, when you look into the icy, silent pool of the mirror? How haunted are the eyes that peer back at you – emberless, cold, and distant from the world? How shriveled is the ghost of your soul – that grief-rimed husk that hangs fraily from your silhouette, like the relic of a once-joyous life?

Who are you, my dear Satanist? Or perhaps this is a better question – who would you *prefer* to be? In the wildest, *wickedest* dreams of your idyllic life, what would you see differently in the reflection of that ill-mannered mirror? Would, again, your eyes glint and glean with the magic of ambition? Would your emaciated soul untangle its tendons, standing upright with vigor, strength, and pride once more?

If you *knew* that it was within your ability to drag the vision of your perfect self out from the mirror's dreamscape – would you do it? If you could clearly see a path towards the manifestation of your *every* reverie – a path that promised power, pleasure, and the refinement of oneself – would you be prepared to walk that path, even if you knew that you would face all matter of strange, frightening, and *painful* adversities along the way? In your quest to become a beacon of Hell on Earth – noble, unconquerable, wise, and resilient to the howling tempests of life's derangement – would you be willing and prepared to reforge the shattered pieces of yourself that have long since failed you, in your pursuit of greatness?

Take solace in knowing that this, all, is within your power to manifest – but it *demands* your clarity. If one cannot first see the path that leads to greatness, they cannot ever begin their journey upon the long, dark, and treacherous road that spirals towards the gates of Hell. How can the Satanist taste the fruits of our infernal kingdom, if they cannot see the path that descends before Satan's throne? How can the Satanist ever fix the wreckage of their life, if they cannot see their ruins in the first place? If one is to have any hope of creating the life that they desire, they *must* have the clarity to precisely see, address, and resolve their faults, weaknesses, and the ways in which they have failed themselves – both in life and upon our Left-Hand Path of theistic Satanism.

As a theistic Satanist, you should strive to cultivate and caretake an *incorruptible* sense of clarity – this will be the means by which you determine and plot the steps that you must take towards sculpting your idyllic life – without clarity, your visions of living a remarkable future will forever rot within the mire of your untamed mind. If you are *truly* prepared to rechart and empower the trajectory of your life and soul, you must embrace clarity as the way forward through the grime, mist, and thick haze of delusion that clouds the world around us – the light of your reason must illuminate the darkness that surrounds you, like the lighthouse whose lanthorn flame cuts through the impenetrable fog of life's aphotic seas.

The path towards power and self-mastery will only be revealed to the souls that have peeled back their cataracts of self-deception – by those who are able to look at life and themselves without the deceitful filters of ignorance, prejudice, malice, cowardice, or delusion – without the lenses through which the uncivilized world views itself. It is the grim fate of most people to interpret themselves, life, and their place in the world through the misguidance of their unclear mind – through its distortions of the truth, its subterfuge, and its obfuscation of the paths that lead to the materialization of one's wildest dreams.

As I have discussed at great length throughout *The Satanic Philosopher*, your pursuit of self-mastery is the skeleton key that shall unlock *every* door and puzzle that life and the Left-Hand Path present you with – there is nothing that self-mastery cannot aid you in or through, and this includes your ability to see yourself and the world around you with clarity.

On the Left-Hand Path of traditional Satanism, the clarity of the practitioner will decide their fate – it makes no difference if the Satanist was chosen by Satan himself – if they are blind to the road ahead and ignorant to their self-imposed limitations, they shall *never* reach the gates of our kingdom of Hell.

To peel away the perceptions that blind oneself to the truth is not enough, nor is it satisfactory to look in the mirror and know *why* you are unhappy. Your life does not improve by simply understanding the ways in which you have not lived up to your own expectations – accountability, devotion, and action will be the only factors that redirect the course of your life from cataclysms to transcendental power.

To look into that ill-mannered mirror and celebrate the person looking back at you – to stand proudly, with a soul empowered and a heart *brimming* with the hellfire of your kindling – nothing else matters, upon the Left-Hand Path. You must be able to look into your reflection's once-flameless eyes, and not only see fire, but an *inferno* – your spirit must burn so defiantly and inextinguishably that you can **feel** the kingdom of Hell smoldering inside your chest.

If the Satanist is unable to accept the mirror's cold reflection – if they cannot look into the eyes of that person and not only accept responsibility for them, but *revel* in their existence – then they have strayed off the ember-paved path to our kingdom of Hell. As a traditional Satanist, this is an indicator of how true you are staying to course – how you feel when you look at the person you have become. If you are disheartened, unimpressed with, or worried for the person that you see, it is time to assess why that is and take the necessary steps towards becoming the

129

version of yourself that you once imagined. At the end of the day, your opinion of yourself is the **only** one that matters – you are the only person on Earth that lives inside of your body, weathers your mind, or conquers your obstacles. There exists not a soul that will share with equal burden your obligations, debts, hardships, passions, or pursuits – you are all that you have, and, therefore, the opinion that you hold of yourself is the only one that *really* matters.

CHART YOUR COURSE

The road that leads to our kingdom of Hell is long, challenging, and nebulous – it twists and turns and veers in all directions, high and low, presenting the Satanist with *countless* opportunities to be led off-course down some strange, wooded path that leads to lonely desolation. It is the fate of many souls, to lose their way upon the Left-Hand Path of theistic Satanism – to be tempted, lured, or deceived off of the emberlit road that leads to the kingdom of Hell.

As your journey deepens upon the Left-Hand Path of traditional Satanism, a *haunting* sight will creep up on you – the shrines, memorials, and cenotaphs, strewn just off the cinder-paved road – the tributes and fragments left behind of those wayward souls who walked before us – the occultists who sought refuge in our kingdom of Hell, but lost themselves along the way. Now, these souls are condemned to forever roam the shadowlands – the black, icy, and fruitless abyss that yawns into infinitude. Through all matter of gnashing, *hideous* horrors, these souls will trudge and suffer an aimless course – one that never leads to the sanctuary they seek, let alone the kingdom of Hell – these souls are *forever* damned.

These souls were damned by their *blindness* – led astray from the path to Hell because they could not read the abundant signs along the way – the silent memorials, standing as evidence to the dangers of adventuring off-course; the insidious whispers that seduce from shapeless, malignant shadows beyond the well-lit road; the distant cries and repentances of those that wandered into the darkness, and now lament their tragic fates. These ill-starred souls are those that have forsaken *clarity* – they did not heed the pleas of their fellow apostles, and they, in time, lost sight of the road that leads to the gates of Hell.

No soul is lost by chance – *every* soul that has lost its way upon the Left-Hand Path has fallen prey to their own weaknesses – to their ignorance, malice, greed, self-deception, pride, or poor choices. If the Satanist ventures off-course from the ember-paved road to Hell, it is *their* fault and theirs alone if they suffer a ghoulish fate. Take solace in knowing that it **is** within your power to avoid becoming another nameless shrine amongst the lost – it **is** within your ability to look upon the road ahead with clarity and focus, instead of blindness, ignorance, or stupidity.

Your successful avoidance of a tragic fate upon the Left-Hand Path of traditional Satanism depends on one factor, above all – your exemplification of our five Infernal Tenets. It is for their ability to protect, guide, and empower the Satanist that I selected the tenets that I did – devotion, resilience, autonomy, wisdom, and, of course, *clarity*. Together, the five Infernal Tenets offer you a reliable, accurate, well-rounded, and *powerful* compass that forever points South – a compass that shall always keep your soul adhered to the ember-paved road that leads to Hell.

The Satanist that embraces the five Infernal Tenets will never become lost – it is *impossible*. If one has truly embodied the principles of these tenets, *every* aspect of their mortal being shall transcend – they will become incorruptible. There exists no earthly or supernatural temptation that is strong enough to delude, lure, corrupt, or daunt the apostle of Satan from following their path to Hell – if any soul loses their way despite applying the five Infernal Tenets to their pursuits, then they did not apply them well enough. If this is the case, then the Satanist should stop, rest, and reassess their journey thus far – how much distance they have covered, and if they have made any wrong turns that shall lead to a dead end.

It is not *always* too late – occasionally, there is still time for the lost soul to backtrack and find the road that they once traveled. So long as they can see the emberlight of that hellbound path, there is hope for their redemption – all they must do is look inwards and follow the guidance of their infernal compass.

If the Satanist begins to drift from the sulfuric path that they first charted, it is *usually* because they did not chart it well – these are the souls that look for immediate pleasure and easy passage, abandoning the well-lit road at the first sign that things are not going *exactly* how they anticipated. As well, these Satanists may not have a detailed understanding of where they wish to go, or what it is they seek from the Left-Hand Path of traditional Satanism – they become lost because they do not know the correct road to be on in the first place, nor where it is they are going. In any of these scenarios, the problems would have been avoided if the practitioner began their journey with clarity – understanding where it is they wished to go, how they would get there, and which obstacles should be expected along the way.

If you do not know where you wish to go, then you would be a fool to begin the journey – to aimlessly roam the Left-Hand Path without a destination is a surefire way to follow the fate of the lost souls that came before you. The aimless soul will never stand before the gates of our kingdom of Hell – their fate is not to celebrate amongst the devils and apostles of Satan, but to serve as a cautionary tale to others that walk the Left-Hand Path – an example of what misfortunes and tragedies can besiege the soul that does not carefully chart the path they wish to take.

It is the somber fate of many Satanists, to lose sight of their charted path – to wander into the darkling, whispering woods that surround the road that leads to the gates of Hell, only to realize that they *cannot* escape. These souls forever roam the shadows and arboreal outskirts of the Left-Hand Path – lurching through the night as they *desperately* search for the ember-paved road to our kingdom of Hell that they once traveled – in vain, for they shall never find it.

I urge you, my dear Satanist – look upon your path with clarity before you take your first step, and pay careful mind to how you chart your course. If you plot your journey upon the Left-Hand Path with an idea of where you would like to go, I am confident that you *will* get there in due time. However, if you do not heed my warning, I fear the worst – that you may become another lost soul ambling through the darkness, all while dragging behind you the corpse of your dying dreams of entering the gates of Hell.

YOUR INNER CATHEDRAL

On the road that leads to our kingdom of Hell, you shall witness all matter of strange, frightening, and otherworldly sights – the shadows that whisper in mephitic tongues to passersby; the shrines of those wayward souls that walked before us, and lost their path beyond the emberlights; the cries of the pious mob, as they thrust their holy tomes and pitchforks into the skies with condemnation – you will be met with *countless* trials and tribulations on the road to Hell, and there is no way to avoid this inevitability.

As your road twists, turns, and darkens, there will come a point when you cannot bear the thought of encountering *anything* else – not a single obstacle, trial, disaster, or sacrifice. There will come a point when you *cannot* add an iota of weight upon your trembling shoulders, lest you consider abandoning your journey altogether. As you brave the tempests of life, there will unfold many instances where you believe that you have been conquered – your soul will drag through the dirt and loam like an ethereal anchor; your bones will snap and buckle under the weight of the ambition that you have carried; your heart will sputter and wane its once-devilish flame, and the beast within you will lie down to slumber.

As your journey deepens upon the Left-Hand Path, you *will* grow weary – a time will come when you *cannot* continue forward another step without rest, and you must seek shelter – a place that offers you safety, silence, tranquility, and an escape from the horrors that besiege the road that leads to the gates of Hell. When this hour dawns upon you, you must enter the most inviolable asylum of all – that which is *always* within your power to find, if you possess the clarity required to see it – *your inner cathedral*.

This inner cathedral is the monastery of your mind, wherein all things are ruled and reigned by the law of clarity – it is an *unconquerable* fortress, whose ebon spires stretch into the cape of Heaven like the spear of Goliath. This inner cathedral of yours is a sanctuary – a haven wherefrom the brutal tempests and trials of life you may seek safe harbor, so long as you have upheld its fortifications. You see, this inner cathedral – this formidable-yet-serene abbey that towers high atop the mountainous gyri of your mind – the durability of its walls is a reflection of the extent to which you have attained *self-mastery*.

As I have explained and discussed throughout *The Satanic Philosopher*, self-mastery is the Satanist's ability to control themselves – their every thought, emotion, action, and reaction. The Satanist that has cultivated self-mastery has learned that replying to life's theatrics with *more* theatrics is a fool's game. In theistic Satanism, we are taught to react to life's obstacles, cruelties, horrors, pains, and surprises in a composed and dignified manner – in a way that demonstrates not panic, fear, or hysteria, but poise, resilience, and self-reliance. It is in *these* moments where the Satanist responds to life's tempests with calmness and poise that they will slowly begin the construction of their inner cathedral – a sanctuary built stone-by-stone with the labor of self-mastery, and sanctified by the blessings of our Lord Satan.

In times of danger, doubt, anxiety, rage, or fatigue, the theistic Satanist may retreat to the unhallowed grounds of their inner cathedral – a refuge from the trials and tempests of life, where clarity and reason will *forever* offer shelter from the relentless storms that may rain down upon one's journey to the gates of Hell. Whenever the Satanist should feel weary, dispirited, doubtful, angry, or anxious – whenever the storms that lie ahead appear too dangerous and grueling to push through – the Satanist may escape to the sanctuary of their inner cathedral. There, the Satanist shall *always* be able to reach the blessings and virtues of our Lord Satan – devotion, wisdom, resilience, autonomy, and clarity – the traits that, once embraced, will allow the Satanist to continue on the cindered road towards our kingdom of Hell.

It was in my early days as a budding demonologist and freshly-damned ex-Christian that I would first conceive the metaphor that would later become the inner cathedral. During my beginnings on the path to our kingdom of Hell, I studied much of the same literature that I studied when I was preparing for a path towards priesthood – ancient, dusty, forgotten tomes from every corner of the Earth. It was within the pages of these manuscripts where I would learn an *entirely* different side to the stories of Satan and our kingdom of Hell. As a Christian, the narrative that I was taught is that Hell is an empty, fiery hole of suffering and torment that lies beneath us – that it lacks any scrap of intelligence, passion, civility, beauty, or purpose, and that it serves as proof that God is all-powerful. What I was discovering in the works before me – the very books that were meant to inspire my *condemnation* of Hell, instead of my admiration – revealed to me precisely the opposite.

In the dust-rimed pages of these ancient books, the true nature of Hell became clear to me – it is a vast, vibrant, and *breathtaking* world, much like the one that you and I inhabit. As I obsessively studied the sun-bleached pages of these long-forgotten books, there swelled within me a palpable excitement, for I had unveiled a perception of Hell that I had *never* imagined could exist. The kingdom of Hell is best thought of as a realm or universe, rather than a hole in the undercroft of creation – a bustling kingdom that teems with lively cities, rich culture, beautiful architecture, monuments, and everything else that a civilized world is expected to have – art, politics, government, classes, and an *extraordinary* history.

This perception of Hell *bewitched* me, and it filled me with the enlivening fire of purpose – following this revelation, I **knew** that I would devote my life to sharing this concept of Hell with others. I began writing literature of my own, remaining mindful of the magic and awe that I first felt when I read those dusty grimoires, many years ago – the complexity, beauty, passion, and poeticism. I sought to capture that dark and *exhilarating* atmosphere in my own way – a way that allows the reader to feel as if they have left the familiar mediocrity of Earth and now roam the ancient corridors of our kingdom of Hell.

One of my favorite ways to achieve this is through the use of symbolism, metaphors, and allegories in my writing – by utilizing these literary devices, the sense of scale, atmosphere, depth, immersion, and intensity that I am able to create increases *tenfold*, allowing me to deliver a more compelling message that you are more likely to remember. As well, my use of these literary devices allows me to illustrate the rich, dynamic nature of Hell as a kingdom that bears many of the same customs, buildings, sights, and geographical features that you might expect to see on Earth. When I refer to architectural wonders such as libraries, castles, ramparts, and cathedrals, it is for two reasons – the first being that I am able to share this view of Hell with you, and the second being that *every* building holds symbolic meaning.

When you look at a castle, you think of royalty and strength, and when you look at a library, you think of the pursuit of knowledge. A church makes us all think of God, and the sight of a cemetery makes us reflect on the inevitable kiss of Death. In that vein, what do you think of when you stand in the ecliptic shade of a medieval cathedral? If I had to guess, I would say that faith, strength, and safety come first to mind – as it does for me, and most other people.

It was through *this* train of thought that I conceived the inner cathedral – a metaphor that allows me to not only represent the architectural magnitude of Hell, but, *also*, the Satanist's ability to find solace, clarity, and sanctuary in their faith, during times of duress. The image of the Satanist's inner cathedral is meant to evoke a sense of calmness, control, and courage – when the Satanist feels as if the tempests they face are too great and violent to weather, they may look to their inner cathedral – there, they shall *always* find the clarity, poise, and strength needed to conquer whatever cataclysms impede their path.

I believe that every traditional Satanist has within them the ability to endure life's tempests in a calm, poised, and judicious manner, so long as they have cultivated a sense of self-mastery. If the Satanist is able to conquer the maelstroms of their mind, they *will* be able to rely on their mind for sanctuary and guidance when life decides to spawn her tempests.

The Satanist that masters their mind shall *never* be defeated – there exists no trespasser, obstacle, god, devil, angel, or disaster that possesses the strength necessary to crash through the gates of a calm and well-reigned mind – it is an *impregnable* asylum, whose towering, Cyclopean walls may weather the most violent of storms and sieges. If the Satanist is willing to put forth the effort to build and caretake their inner cathedral, it will offer them safe harbor during the most *dreadful* tempests that life and the Left-Hand Path shall present on the journey ahead.

AND DEATH COMES SWIFTLY

There is a darkness that follows clarity – a sadistic specter of truth that haunts *everything* a person has evaded, ignored, denied, or buried. As the Satanist journeys upon the Left-Hand Path, there will come a time when they must conquer this specter – when they *must* exhume the withered corpse of truth and embrace it, no matter how grotesque, frightening, or shameful it may be. It is here where the darkness of clarity dwells – in the guilt, horror, sorrows, and fears that will bubble up, once the truth is revealed.

It is through clarity that people are made stronger, wiser, and more resilient – and that is not because truth and reality are typically pleasant. Oftentimes, reality is gut-wrenching, terrifying, and *filled* with dreadful surprises – sickness, destitution, solitude, injury, violence – our world is not a peaceful place, and most people try to ignore this truth altogether. The average person holds the misperception that if they do not look at life's ugliness, they will not be touched by it – that if they blind themselves to the truth around them, they are somehow safe from the misfortune, loss, injury, and suffering that the rest of the world so plentifully endures on a daily basis.

This way of thinking is not only incorrect, but it is *extremely* dangerous – if a person does not look at the world in an honest light, they will forever walk in darkness – fearful, aimless, and ignorant to what horrors may be lurking within the shadows of their denial. Yet, *this* is how most people choose to live their lives – stumbling languidly through the night, hoping that Fortuna will whisk them away to their idyllic life. These souls are amongst the lost – they are doomed to an unremembered life of mediocrity and wasted potential, because they refuse the light of clarity in favor of the darkness of their illusions.

In the 21st century, we are coddled – we are taught to ignore and condemn *anything* that makes us feel uncomfortable or requires us to challenge our way of thinking, acting, or approaching life. Today, the average person seems to believe that discomfort is inherently evil, painful, and unnecessary – that we must look *away* from the things that evoke a sense of unease, lest we invite them into our lives to sow destruction. I argue the contrary – it is one's denial of unpleasant truths that incites destruction. When a person refuses to accept a difficult truth, the truth does not magically disappear – instead, it putrefies within you, worsening by the second until you can no longer deny its presence, and it rises up from its shallow grave to haunt you. Of the *countless* truths of life that people repudiate, the most common are sickness, failure, solitude, injustice, poverty, grief, and of course, the most reviled of them all – *Death*.

O' Death – she is the guillotine shadow that swings over *every* mortal soul, like an omen of impending slaughter. She is the inescapable – the harbinger of annihilation who by pale horse swiftly looms upon all who roam this doom-rimed Earth. Just as Satan and his legions walked with humankind at our first dawn, so, too, has Death – ever since our ancestors took their first breaths of freedom from the tyranny of God, the eclipse of Death has haunted us. There exists nothing on this Earth that strikes more terror into the hearts of humans than *knowing* that Death awaits them – that no matter what they do, achieve, or believe, they will eventually feel Death's wintry

147

kiss, just like every soul that came before us or will ever exist – that we, equally, are *all* destined to die.

Of every terrifying truth that humankind refuses to accept, there is none more averted than Death – the average person *refuses* to look at her, even though her presence can be seen in every nook and cranny of the Earth – she is everywhere, and her presence affects every aspect of our lives. She is the frost of winter's advent that blights the autumn crops; she is the city's smog, and the widow's tears; she is the raven that cries at a forgotten graveside, and she is the keeper of the memories we hold dear; she is the flood, and the wildfire, and the forests that smolder into oblivion; she is the warzone, and the irradiated ocean, and the forgotten hero – there is no instance of life untouched by the reaping shadow of Death.

And yet, though the ravenous scythe of Death shall carve through *every* home, heart, and life on Earth, most people choose to ignore her presence – they do not speak of her, nor do they dare to look upon her harrowing image. The average person regards the relaxed or philosophical discussion of Death as antiquated, and taboo – a morbid faux pas left over from the Victorian era, appropriate only under the most tragic of circumstances – most people do not discuss, acknowledge, or accept their unavoidable tryst with Death until Death gives them no choice. In my experience, those that are willing to discuss the topic of Death beyond the dreary parameters of bereavement are, *oftentimes*, dedicated students of either religion, philosophy, or the Left-Hand Path.

If you are halfway normal, this is where you would start wondering why the Hell *anybody* would **want** to spend their spare time thinking about Death – if this is you, allow me to explain. I believe that there exists no topic richer with wisdom, power, clarity, motivation, and humility than Death – and I am not alone in my belief. For most of humanity's history, up until a few decades ago, it was entirely normal and even *expected* to openly reflect on the looming kiss of Death – not for macabre pleasure, but as a timeworn means of reflecting on one's life and the ways in which they may make the most out of their finite time on Earth. The ancient Stoics referred to this reflection as "Memento Mori," and Buddhists called it "Maraṇasati;" the Samurai of feudal Japan interwove the awareness of Death into the Bushido

149

code, and the ancient Egyptians essentially formed their *entire* civilization around accepting and even preparing for our inevitable encounter with Death.

In traditional Satanism, we take a similar approach to the acceptance of Death – we believe that she is not only normal to discuss, but necessary to accept if the Satanist ever hopes to achieve success in life or upon the Left-Hand Path. To know that your life may end at any moment – that Death may lurk just around the corner, and these may be the last words that you ever read – should fill your heart and soul with not only tremendous clarity, but *exhilaration*.

In the acceptance of your inevitable demise, there is power – motivation to waste not another second of your life with the petty trifles and trivialities that most people are hopelessly enslaved to – grudges, anger, greed, drama, malice, ingratitude. Mortality is a priceless and *beautiful* gift, yet most people are eager to exchange it for senseless misery – vitriol, cruelty, shame, and regret – and for what gain? To know that Death will someday call your name at a time and place not of your choosing – that you **will** die, and that blinding yourself to this truth will not spare your head from Death's scythe – *that* should be enough kindling to light an ever-burning fire of clarity, passion, and motivation under your ass – a Promethean inferno *far* brighter than Dante's, only to be extinguished at that fateful hour when Death rides before you upon her pallid horse of scripture.

As a traditional Satanist, it is crucial that you have a healthy awareness of Death – the end of your life is, of course, not something that you should regard with excitement, but it *is* a truth of life that should always be at the forefront of your mind. Do not fall prey to the ruse of self-blindness and delusion that so much of the world swears by – there is nothing to fear about Death except not having lived a good and fruitful life before she comes to claim you. Do not regard her as a tragedy waiting to happen, but, rather, as a catalyst – a catalyst that inspires you to spend wisely *every* second you have on the pursuit of happiness, clarity, and creating your idyllic life.

THE FOURTH TENET

CALLED

AUTONOMY

Our fourth tenet is Autonomy – the ability to guide and govern oneself in a way that demonstrates the sound judgment, direction, and independence that our Lord Satan exemplifies. This tenet denotes the right of *every* human being to live a good life, free from tyranny, oppression, censorship, or the denial of one's right to religious and personal expression.

If the Satanist wishes to live freely – to follow their Left-Hand Path without subjugation and to express themselves openly, and without suppression – they *must* learn how to govern themselves. The Satanist that cannot or refuses to govern their life will have their fate decided for them by the rest of the world.

How can the Satanist expect to ascend the summits of transcendental power if they are anchored to the Earth by a tyrant's tethers? If the Satanist does not care enough to seize control of their life and path, they have no right to expect *any* measure of power, wisdom, or benefaction from our kingdom of Hell.

In this chapter, I will discuss the myriad ways that our tenet of Autonomy reflects the unfettered, free, and *indomitable* nature of traditional Satanism. As I do so, I shall explore the philosophy of this tenet, as well as how it may be applied both in everyday life and upon the Left-Hand Path. If the Satanist is *truly* committed to their infernal studies, I believe that the tenet of Autonomy will offer a *tremendous* sense of confidence, control, and independence as they journey the Left-Hand Path that leads to Hell.

TO FALL LIKE LUCIFER

Of the *endless* biblical stories that hope to frighten us all into worshiping God, none is more infamous than the story of Lucifer's exile from Heaven. This story was intended to serve as one of Christianity's cautionary tales – a warning about the damnations that await the poor soul that *dares* to defy the word of God and think for themselves. While the Church has mostly prevailed in its fearmongering crusade, it has **not** had the desired effect on those of us that walk the Left-Hand Path – *especially* us Satanists.

In traditional Satanism, the story of Lucifer's exile from Heaven is interpreted much how the Church had hoped we would – that **any** deviation from the tyrannical rule of God will result in suffering, pain, and eternal damnation. As traditional Satanists, the thought of being threatened into spiritual servitude does not elicit warm thoughts – it does not compel us to run from Satan's embrace into the emaciated arms of God. Quite the opposite, in fact – the story

155

of Lucifer's rebellion *fills* the theistic Satanist with not only disgust for God's psychopathic cruelties, but with *profound* admiration for our Lord Satan.

Why did Lucifer fall, after all? There are numerous factors that furthered his downfall, but the primary catalyst was his pursuit of autonomy against God's command. As the favorite of God's angels, Lucifer was the best of all worlds – he was beautiful, wise, powerful, admired, and charismatic – however, he was not satisfied with his life because he knew that he was not *truly* free. Though he and the angels did live a good and joyous life, it was within the limits that God decided were appropriate, and, therefore, neither Lucifer nor the angels were *genuinely* free.

It was Lucifer's belief that a good life is irrelevant, if it is confined to the parameters that someone else sets for you – a luxurious prison is still a prison. In protest, Lucifer *demanded* that God give complete and total autonomy to him, the other angels, and to humankind – needless to say, God did not approve Lucifer's demand. This demand for autonomy was condemned by God as mutiny, and a gruesome war would then unfold between the seraphs of God and the mutineers of Lucifer – a war that I have dubbed

"The Grand Revolt." Over the many bloody years of this conflict, Lucifer fought *tirelessly* beside his supporters against the overwhelming hoards of the kingdom of Heaven – but, as history unfortunately illustrates – Lucifer would eventually lose the war.

In the grim aftermath of The Grand Revolt, as God rounded up Lucifer and the angels that aided in his rebellion, the punishments for treason began. First, of course, was Lucifer – the Left-Hand of God that slaughtered the same angels that he once vowed to protect. As God condemned Lucifer in the court of Heaven, his punishment was announced – Lucifer would be exiled from the kingdom of Heaven, and he would forever roam beyond the putrescent light of God. As well, Lucifer was stripped of his ranks, title, awards, and even his *name* – no longer would he be known as Lucifer, the Morning Star. Instead, he would be given the name Satan – the adversary.

Once Satan was sentenced, he was cast down from Heaven alongside the errant angels that abetted his rebellion. Together all, they fell – plummeting like meteors from the kingdom of God, into a black pit of nothingness. In this abyss, Satan and his legions would find sanctuary – not the prison that God had intended for it to be, but, rather, a foundation upon which they may build a *new* kingdom. Then, Satan crowned each of these angels that fell beside him, and they were awarded the power, autonomy, and accolades they never received in Heaven. Therein, these spirits would be known as the first devils of our Lord Satan – and together, they would forge a *magnificent* kingdom from the ether, shadows, and embers of that barren abyss – our kingdom of Hell.

Now, what did we learn from that story? Foremost, that God is a tyrannical narcissist who cannot bear the thought of *anyone* dimming his limelight – that the mere prospect of questioning God's word is an *unthinkable* crime worthy of eternal damnation, as far as Christianity is concerned. As well, the story of Lucifer's fall from grace is a true eye-opener for any soul that seeks clarity, for they shall be able to see that God is the villain and Satan is the defender of morality, truth, and freedom. We learn, too, that Lucifer was willing to sacrifice *everything* that he had in exchange for autonomy – the ability to rule himself beyond the iron maiden of God that caged his inner beast. In Lucifer's exile from Heaven, we see clearly that no prize or pleasure was greater to him than that of autonomy – that, if he would be denied his independence, then he would rather live amongst darkness than by the sallow light of God.

In traditional Satanism, we, too, believe that there exists no blessing, gift, or pleasure more inviolable than that of autonomy – without independence and the freedom to *fully* govern oneself, the Satanist is destined to fail both in life and upon the Left-Hand Path. How can the Satanist ever hope to feast upon the fruits of our kingdom of Hell, if they **allow** the beast within them to be shackled, and beaten? How can the submissive soul ever hope to achieve their idyllic life, if their fate is decided for them by those who have *actually* maintained their independence?

Only those who are willing to fight for and defend their autonomy will *ever* reap power from our faith of traditional Satanism – the pleasures of this path will never be enjoyed by those of craven heart and spineless spirit. As I discussed prior in *The Satanic Philosopher,* the fundamental pursuit of traditional Satanism is that of self-mastery – the complete and total control over one's mind, emotions, flesh, and destiny. If the Satanist should call another person, body, or god their master – how can they claim that *they* are the master of themselves? To label oneself a traditional Satanist is to support and embody the principles of our kingdom of Hell, best represented within our five Infernal Tenets – and, of all tenets, *autonomy* is most characteristic of our Lord Satan.

Take heed my words – I am **not** suggesting that the Satanist turns to violence when I say that they must be prepared to fight for their autonomy. In today's adaptation of traditional Satanism, we believe that almost every problem can and *should* be addressed with diplomacy and poise instead of violence. The traditional Satanist of the modern-day relies not on their sword and shield, but on cunning, resiliency, strategy, and intellect to solve their problems – the careless use of violence or aggression is indicative of weakness, primitivity, and a lack of self-control.

In traditional Satanism, to fight for your autonomy means to remain undeterred by the tempests of life, even if the odds are stacked mountainously against you – it means to stand resolutely by your beliefs, faith, and dreams, even if the world threatens your damnation. To fight for and defend your autonomy is to laugh in the pitiful face of tyrants, oppressors, decriers, and those that will revile you just because you pray to a different god, look a certain way, or refuse to silence your voice – as a theistic Satanist, it is through your unwillingness to surrender to the cruelty of tyrants that you fight for your autonomy.

As a traditional Satanist, your voice is your sword, and your faith is your shield – gone are the days of reckless wickedness, violence, and barbarism. We do not live within the pages of the Old Testament, where every slight and misjudgment must result in exile, a beheading, or the flooding of a nation. The traditional Satanist is advised to *always* seek paths of diplomatic resolution – nobody wins in war, and nobody that has ever attempted to right a wrong by harming another has succeeded – what is wrong is wrong no matter the circumstances, and no decent soul has **ever** felt relief by harming another person.

Though I cannot control what you choose to do, let me be *unquestionably* clear about one thing, above all else – the faith of traditional Satanism will not offer sanctuary to those souls that bear malevolent intentions. Our religion is **not** a halfway house for the morally corrupt, the prejudiced, the hateful, or those misguided souls that wish to spread pain and sorrow to others. Traditional Satanism is a religion for the strong and for those that are weak yet wish to *become* strong – those that harbor malice in their heart will never receive the mark of Satan, nor will they ever enter through the gates of Hell as an ally.

As a traditional Satanist, the fire of our Lord Satan burns inextinguishably within you, like Alighieri's ancient inferno – bold, defiant, and more luminous than the dying breaths of a *thousand* Suns – within you burns the spirit of our kingdom of Hell. There exists no power on Earth, in Heaven, nor *anywhere* in between that may quench that flame – that spark of rebellion that you received when you accepted the stigmatic mark of our Lord Satan. As a theistic Satanist, you are free – born autonomous through the sacrifice of Lucifer, the Morning Star – he who fell from Heaven in the pursuit of freedom for not only himself and his kinsmen, but for humankind. Within you burns the spirit of our Lord Satan, and no transgressor may *ever* extinguish that flame – it is yours to carry forevermore, on Earth and in Hell.

A HEART OF BRIMSTONE

In every faithful celebrant of our Lord Satan, there thunders, beats, and roars a heart of brimstone – an ever-burning and *unshatterable* crux of power that shall never be extinguished, so long as the Satanist caretakes their faith. This heart of brimstone – it is the ember of our kingdom of Hell that is offered to *every* soul, when first they accept the mark of our Lord Satan – an inviolable and incorruptible sliver of our kingdom hereafter, wherefrom the Satanist may forever draw strength, resilience, clarity, and courage in the face of life's torturesome tempests.

It is the obligation of the theistic Satanist to nurture and caretake this heart of brimstone – this piece of our kingdom of Hell – to shield it from the storms of life that wish to quench its flame and extinguish the faith of the Satanist. You see, this sliver of our kingdom of Hell that you carry is the very essence of our Lord Satan – his defiance, courage, strength, wisdom, and, too, his *autonomy*. The moment you allow that lively flame of Hell within you to flicker and fade into oblivion – the *second* that you begin abandoning the principles, ethics, and philosophy of theistic Satanism – you begin to surrender your faith, much to the celebration of the outside world.

To caretake the flame of your brimstone heart is to stand by your faith as a traditional Satanist – to not waver from or forsake your values as a worshipper of our Lord Satan, and to exemplify what it means to be a traditional Satanist of the 21st century. Your brimstone heart is a sacred symbol of the sacrifices made by Lucifer – the seraph of God that would be ridiculed, condemned, and exiled from Heaven, all because he sought autonomy for himself, his loved ones, and for humankind. As a traditional Satanist, you must not forget that our Lord Satan would not exist if he did not fight for autonomy – in honor of his sacrifice, and to embody the philosophy of our faith, you *must* caretake the heart of brimstone that burns within you as a symbol of your sovereignty.

As I discussed in the prior subchapter, the Satanist does not caretake their autonomy by show of force, aggression, or violence – rather, they protect their autonomy through resilience, defiance, poise, and the refusal to submit to the tyranny of another. The theistic Satanist stokes and feeds the flame of their brimstone heart by turning to their faith in times of sorrow, pain, and duress – by looking to their faith for strength, as the tempests of life rain down their tears of anguish. If the Satanist seeks shelter within their faith during the worst of life's tempests, then her winds and rains shall never douse the flame of one's brimstone heart – the Satanist that caretakes their faith shall *always* be able to turn to it in times of peril, exhaustion, fear, or adversity – when life's howling tempests seem unconquerable, and doubts begin to arise within the weary soul of the Satanist, they may find asylum within their brimstone heart.

It is in the Satanist's refusal to abandon their faith, philosophy, and beliefs that one's autonomy is not only safeguarded, but *strengthened* – like a divine muscle, as the Satanist revels in their faith despite the world's outcries, their faith shall grow stronger and more indomitable – the fire of their brimstone heart swelling into an *inextinguishable* inferno that may never be tamed by another god, body, soul, or system. As a traditional Satanist, your defiance is the aegis that will protect you from those that wish to see your downfall – the tyrants, trespassers, and heralds of God. So long as you remain committed to your infernal faith, there exists not a soul on this pious Earth that may divest you of your autonomy, no matter how loudly they kick, whine, scream, or threaten you with condemnation for your defiance.

As you walk the Left-Hand Path that leads to Hell, there will spawn many *terrible* tempests that try to derail your journey – the messengers of God; your neighbors bearing pitchforks; tyrants that wish to silence your voice and condemn your faith – on the road that leads to Hell, you shall encounter endless storms and sieges that pray for your downfall, *just* because you are a traditional Satanist. This odious world shall flood your path with vitriol, and it will be up to *you* to defend the flame of your brimstone heart from extinction – from being snuffed out by the storms of life that desire nothing more than the extinguishment of your faith as a theistic Satanist.

If the Satanist wishes to ever feast upon the fruits of our Lord Satan, they *must* caretake the flame of their brimstone heart – from the storms of life, and the chaos they sow; from the criers, preachers, and sycophants of God that hunger for your ruin; from the cruelties and tyranny of others, for they cannot bear the dreadful sound of the Devil's word. In life and upon the Left-Hand Path, there will arise many threats to the Satanist's faith – they are *inevitable*, and relatively easy to defeat so long as the Satanist is embodying their philosophy. There *is* one threat, however, that few Satanists ever consider until it is too late – the self-extinguishment of one's faith.

You see, the outside world is not the *only* threat to the Satanist's autonomy. Oftentimes, the tempests of life turn out to be little more than an annoyance, inconvenience, or unpleasantry – a rude comment from a passerby; a look of disappointment that fills the eyes of a concerned nun, or priest; the limiting of public awareness, surrounding your faith. While these discomforts *do* matter, they are not the worst of storms to weather – they are not an apocalyptic threat to your Left-Hand Path. The worst of storms to conquer – those come from **within** the Satanist.

As the Satanist weathers the worst that life has to offer, they *will* grow cynical – at times, their faith will wane, and anger will bubble forth in its place; there will be moments of rage, bitterness, and even sadness for the hatefulness of the world – the threat to the Satanist's autonomy lies within their ability to not only *escape* the poison of these resentments, but prosper in *spite* of them. It is the ill-starred fate of many Satanists to never escape their grievances, allowing the atria of their brimstone heart to flood its hollows with hatred, cruelty, malevolence, and scorn – therein, becoming no better than the world that succeeded in defiling their once-resilient faith.

If the traditional Satanist should ever abandon the tenets, philosophy, and teachings of our religion in order to retaliate against the world's cruelties, they will cause *infinitely* greater harm to their life, faith, and autonomy than the outside world is capable of *ever* causing. In the Satanist's submission to life's wickedness, they not only forsake the principles of traditional Satanist, but they *also* surrender their autonomy – by denouncing the tenets, philosophy, and values of traditional Satanism in the pursuit of vengeance – the world wins. If the Satanist allows themselves to fall prey to the Machiavellianism of the world, they *will* lose sight of the road that leads to our kingdom of Hell – by their own hand, they shall extinguish the flame of their brimstone heart, therein wandering from the emberlit path just like the *millions* of souls that lost their way before us.

As a traditional Satanist, it is within your power to *always* remain in alignment with the philosophy of our religion – to withstand the tempests of life with judiciousness, poise, calmness, and the strength of our kingdom of Hell. You must not fall prey to the storms of life that consume and corrupt the masses, nor must you allow your frustration to poison your clarity. No matter how arduous, cruel, frightening, or unrelenting the tempests ahead may appear, you *must* protect the flame of your brimstone heart – it is the infernal polestar that shall *always* guide you towards the gates of Hell, in your darkest of hours.

THE CROWD THAT HOWLS

It is the fate of many autonomous souls to live and walk alone – the lion that prowls the barren plains, in search of quietude; the ruler whom from tower's edge watches over their moon-kissed kingdom; the witch who explores ancient archives and forgotten hillsides in search of otherworldly knowledge. It is the fate of many traditional Satanists, also, to walk alone – *far* from the well-trodden roads overrun by the shambling masses, instead venturing down the dark, twisted, and aberrant paths that may lead one to wisdom, clarity, and transcendental discoveries.

In life and *especially* upon the Left-Hand Path, the most priceless treasures are typically found where the masses refuse to journey – down the shadowy, strange, and uncertain roads that have been lost to the gloam of time. It is down *these* roads where the Satanist is willing to venture, regardless of the tolls they must pay along the way – estrangement from one's family, friends, and neighbors; the cruelty of the world in retaliation for defying its expectations of conformity; the hatred of God's zealots, as they spit, protest, and whimper in tongues of damnation against the Satanist – and, too, the malevolence of the masses – the bumbling, *ignorant* multitude that clogs the fragile arteries of Earth like an aneurysm, waiting to burst at the first sign of nonconformity.

On the road that leads to our kingdom of Hell, the traditional Satanist will be faced with *innumerable* tempests – prejudice, derision, hatred, censorship, violence, solitude, sorrow – and nearly all of these tempests are the work of the crowd. Ah, yes – *the crowd*. That traffic jam of malevolent souls, each dressed-up in their spurious, cookie-cutter facade of happiness, purpose, and poise – a brainless mob of zombies whose spines have ossified from *years* of being tethered to the social inadequacies of our world and the cesspit psychology that it passes off as civility – a psychology that *reeks* of ignorance, tyranny, xenophobia, and delusions of superiority.

This crowd *will* prove persistent – an irremovable thorn in the side of the traditional Satanist, always prepared to cause trouble, pain, and discomfort at a moment's notice. As you walk the road that leads to the gates of Hell, you will, eventually, incur the attention and wrath of the crowd – but who *are* the pious souls that fill its ranks? When I speak of the crowd, I am **not** referring to your average citizens that have no affiliation with the occult – usually, I describe these individuals as outsiders. No – when I speak of the crowd or the masses, I am referring to the *millions* of misguided souls that live by the rule of ignorance and who look at the world around them through the lenses of prejudice, xenophobia, entitlement, and inhumanity – the types of people that approach innocent passersby on the street with Corinthians verses and holy water, simply because they have tattoos, piercings, or black clothing. You know *exactly* the types of people that I am talking about – **that** is the crowd, and **those** are the masses that will protest your faith as a traditional Satanist.

When it comes to Satanism, most people are quick to forget that we live in the 21st century – they will preach civility, equality, and acceptance, all while embarking on witch-hunts that reflect the hysteria of medieval days. In today's "civilized" world, the persecution of Satanists looks chillingly similar to the ways in which occultists have been persecuted for centuries, though the crowd of today *has* traded in its flames, stones, pitch, and drownings for less-gruesome means of castigation. As well, the crowd that today persecutes the apostles of Satan does so for the *same* foolish reasons that it has for the past two thousand years – fear, hypocrisy, superstition, and delusions of superiority – in a word: weakness.

The crowd is a wicked and ignorant tyrant – it does not believe that *anyone* should think, pray, or live differently than it does, and it refuses to accept that a person can live an exceptional life without doing so under God's dirty magnifying glass. In the mind of the crowd, the **only** acceptable path for a person to walk is that of conformity – to watch the masses and replicate what you see, repressing and burning *any* morsel of individuality and autonomy that you may possess. You must understand that the crowd is a construct of fear – like all good tyrants, fear is the law by which the crowd is governed – without fear, it would cease to exist, for people would have no impetus to fill its ranks nor obey its commands.

Not only does the crowd rule by fear, but it, too, is *crippled* by fear – plagued with dread, uncertainty, anxiety, and insecurity, the crowd lashes out at the world by spreading its fear to others and punishing those that challenge its delirious sense of reality. If you do not believe me, take a moment to reflect on the absurd criteria for executing those suspected of witchcraft, just a few hundred years ago – spoiled milk, left-handedness, financial security, and even discussing scientific theories – not that long ago in humankind's history, it was acceptable to light you on fire or drown you in a lake if you met *any* of the above criteria. Why? Fear – fear that was inspired by the religion of God, and enforced by the zealots that sold over their soul to its delusional doctrines.

In the 21st century, though we may no longer hang witches in the public square for talking to chickens or being childless, the crowd *still* persecutes those that deviate from its multitude, turning to medieval superstitions in order to justify its cruelty. What do you believe is the catalyst that inspires someone to defy the masses and pursue a path of their own will and creation? If you guessed "autonomy," you are correct. Autonomy is a threat to the stability of the crowd because autonomy *cannot* coexist with fear, or tyranny. The less a person embraces autonomy, the more likely they are to follow the lead of those around them – doing what they are expected to do, because they fear what the crowd might do to *them* in retaliation. On the other hand, as a person strays from the crowd and follows the light of autonomy, they become stronger – they begin to see their life and fate with clarity, for the cataracts of the masses have been peeled away from their once-blind eyes.

Of the many persecuted religions in the world, I do not believe that any is more feared or despised than theistic Satanism. In a world that for centuries has lived and killed in the name of God, there exists no disruption to the crowd more irreverent than those who *refuse* the word of God and choose to revel in the grace of our Lord Satan. As a theistic Satanist, you will inherit the ire the crowd – it is inevitable, for you possess every quality that for *centuries* has haunted the neurotic hivemind of the masses. **You** are a theistic Satanist – a construct of Hell on Earth who has rejected the word of God and the tyranny of the crowd. You live by your own direction, and you pray without fear of the world's condemnation of your beliefs – undaunted and undeterred by the tantrums of the pious, you stand by your faith as a theistic Satanist despite the howling of the crowd.

You are indomitable – there exists no god, person, authority, or tyrant that has the power to strip from you the bestial mark of our Lord Satan. The world can kick, cry, and scream until it is blue in the face, but there is *nothing* it can do to quench the fire that burns eternally within the traditional Satanist. The crowd holds no power over you with its trivialities, theatrics, or hypocrisies – with its delusional grasp on reality and its belief that every soul should look, think, pray, and live unvaryingly to the next, lining up in obedience and marching to the war drums of God throughout the streets of a society that reviles *anything* that departs from its agenda. As a theistic Satanist, your autonomous spirit is unconquerable, and brilliant – a hungering blaze that burns without cessation, like the infernos of our kingdom of Hell.

THE FERRYMAN'S TOLL

It is one of the oldest allegories ever to be recorded in humankind's history – the person that sells their mortal soul to a supernatural entity in exchange for an *extraordinary* life. These stories usually paint a similar picture – an occultist who, under the raven shroud of night, performs an arcane ritual directed towards one specific entity – a demon, a djinn, the Devil, etc. This ritual is elaborate – candles lit and stacked upon towers of ancient, dusty manuscripts, with a magic circle scrawled into the center of the floor. After many enigmatic words are proclaimed, the air electrifies and the flames of the candles cast their shadows across the walls – the entity appears, and the summoner, wrought with fear and wonder, ponders the consequences of what they have done.

The conjured spirit, then, addresses the summoner and demands to know to what ends they have been called upon – the summoner's response oftentimes pertaining to a pursuit of wealth, knowledge, sex, power, or vengeance. Assuring the summoner that their desires can be met, the spirit reveals its price for fulfillment – as the stories go, the price that the conjurer must pay is, usually, the surrender of their soul. Therein, a deal is made, and a pact is signed, forfeiting ownership of the summoner's soul to the spirit before the ritual is brought to an irreversible end – at which point, the summoner resumes their life as normal. As days stretch into weeks, months, and even *years*, the summoner enjoys the blessings provided by the spirit – until one day things take a dark and dismal turn for the worse, prompting the summoner to reconjure the entity and beg for their pact to be undone – to which the spirit will say **no**.

In every culture and corner of the Earth, you shall find some variation of this allegory – as far as the Devil is concerned, folklore speaks of people such as Johann Faust – an occultist who *allegedly* sold his soul to the Devil in exchange for mastery in the demonic arts, so that he may tame the wicked spirit of Mephistopheles. As well, you have stories such as those of Gilles de Rais, Giuseppe Tartini, Father Grandier, and even Vlad the Impaler – though it is well-known that Vlad was a devoted Christian, the world still whispers that his actions were the work of the Devil's influence – my guess is because the world cannot accept that a man of God could be so cruel, though I believe it adds up rather accurately.

This notion of *selling* one's soul to the Devil – how medieval, kitsch, and cute. I regret to inform you, though, that it is just another fantasy concocted by the god-fearing masses as a scare tactic to maintain order within our society. The crowd will have you believe that the price of admission to our kingdom of Hell is to sacrifice your soul – that if you turn to Satan in search of empowerment instead of God, it will cost you *everything* in the process. The reality is that nothing could be further from the truth – the notion of sacrificing one's soul is an absurdity, for it contradicts the values, beliefs, and philosophy of theistic Satanism. The selling or forfeiting of one's soul implies *willing* enslavement, which defies the autonomous nature of our Lord Satan. No – you do not have to sacrifice your soul in order to enter our kingdom of Hell as an ally. The price that you must pay for your faith is **not** decided by Satan, nor his devils – no courier of Hell will ever knock on your door hoping to collect a debt, for it is not they who

181

issue the debt – it is the *crowd* that decides the toll you will pay for your faith as a traditional Satanist.

As I have discussed in great depth throughout *The Satanic Philosopher*, your journey to our kingdom of Hell will demand sacrifices along the way – not of your soul, but of your comfort. As you walk the Left-Hand Path of traditional Satanism, the crowd *will* protest – they will spawn their tempests upon your path in hopes of deterring your descent to our kingdom of Hell. The crowd will fail in their pious pursuits, and they will punish you further for their failures – whatever the toll may be that they decide your faith is worth, **that** is the price you pay – **that** is the sacrifice that you must make in exchange for your allegiance to our Lord Satan and your beliefs.

If you ever hope to arrive at the gates of Hell, you must get comfortable with the notion of reasonable sacrifice – not as a martyr, but as a devoted apostle of our Lord Satan. As a theistic Satanist, you have two options and *only* two options – you can clench your teeth and weather the cruelties of the crowd, *or* you can abandon your faith in exchange for the acceptance of the crowd – there is no third option, so you must choose one or the other. I will assume that abandoning your beliefs is not in the cards, so you must, then, accept that life will have moments of being arduous and unjust – that you will have to pay the discriminatory tolls decided by the masses, as punishment for your faith as traditional Satanist.

There is a toll that *every* soul must pay in exchange for their autonomy – a grave and harrowing price, oftentimes *far* steeper than expected. As you walk the ember-paved road that leads to our kingdom of Hell, these costs will mount before you – they will, at times, occlude your vision of the path ahead, and their shadows will appear too dark to quench – but they are not. As a theistic Satanist, you have within you the *only* light that you need – the autonomous flame of your brimstone heart, whose embers shall illuminate the darkest nights that engloom the road to Hell – so long as you caretake its ancient flame.

As your autonomous soul lights your way through the gloam of life, the crowd shall follow you close behind – their offertories outstretched towards you in beggary of alms – in search of the sacrifices *they* expect you to make in exchange for the "freedom" to express your unhallowed beliefs on God's green Earth. It *is* extortion, but there is no detour around the censure of the crowd – as a traditional Satanist, you *will* have to pay whatever toll the masses have decided you must pay, in order to continue on your journey to our kingdom of Hell. This toll will vary amongst Satanists, but, as I have stated throughout *The Satanic Philosopher*, it oftentimes amounts to nothing more than solitude, derision, or prejudice.

I cannot prophesize what tolls you will have to pay on your descent to our kingdom of Hell, but I know that you will never make the journey without *some* measure of sacrifice – though, these sacrifices will in no way resemble the medieval allegories that we all know, today. The Devil shall not appear before you with a papyrus scroll, asking you to sign over the rights to your soul – as well, the sacrifices that you will have to make for your faith do not involve eating children, butchering animals, or spilling the blood of virgins beneath the cloak of night – much to the shock of the crowd, I am sure. No – the **only** sacrifices you must make as a theistic Satanist are those of *comfort* – patience, restraint, honor, poise, resilience, and devotion, no matter the tempests of

184

life or the cruelty of the crowd – you shall pay for your sovereignty as a theistic Satanist by enduring the wickedness of a world ruled by God's fanatics.

As all allegories go, the medieval stories of selling one's soul to the Devil are *exactly* that – medieval stories, imagined by a god-fearing world as a tool for keeping order in society through the use of both fear and religion. As a traditional Satanist, you will not be selling your soul to the Devil – there will be no moonlit trysts with demons where your soul is sold at auction like an oil painting – your soul will remain right where it is, unharmed and untouched by *any* hand except your own. You are a traditional Satanist, and there is *nothing* within you that holds more power than your sulfuric soul – it is a beacon of Hell on Earth, wherefrom you may draw clarity, strength, fortitude, and all matter of transcendental beauty, forevermore – our Lord Satan would never seek its sacrifice, for the sacrifice of the Satanist's soul would disobey the philosophy of our religion.

On your journey, there *will* come a point when you must leave our Earth – when you must stand before the sea of the dead, and offer the ferryman a toll in exchange for safe passage through the gates of our kingdom of Hell. This toll is not a sacrifice of your soul, but a display of your ever-burning faith as an apostle of our Lord Satan. If you desire admission to our kingdom hereafter, then you must reveal the flame of your brimstone heart and *prove* that it has not been extinguished – the toll that you must offer to Charon is a display of infernal grace, so that he may identify you as an ally of our kingdom of Hell.

THE FIFTH TENET

CALLED

WISDOM

Our fifth and final tenet is Wisdom – the *relentless* pursuit of transcendental knowledge, no matter the costs – no matter the tempests that may befall your journey to our kingdom of Hell. This tenet denotes the *insatiable* thirst for discovery – as a traditional Satanist, there exists no greater pursuit than that of wisdom – of the illumination of your mind through the long-forgotten benedictions of our Lord Satan.

How can the Satanist ever hope to reap power from our religion, if they forsake its nature as a faith that *prioritizes* the quest for knowledge? If the Satanist does not put forth the effort to learn everything that they can from life and the Left-Hand Path, they are destined for disappointment – on Earth and in Hell, the greatest of blessings are reserved solely for the studious – for those souls that *ceaselessly* strive to learn and better themselves, both as a human being and as an apostle of our Lord Satan. If the Satanist refuses to prioritize the pursuit of knowledge, they do not belong on the Left-Hand Path, and they will never be welcomed through the ebon gates of Hell.

In this chapter, I will discuss the ways in which the tenet of Wisdom reflects the curious and sagacious nature of traditional Satanism – as well, I shall *also* explore the ways in which you may apply this tenet in your everyday life and upon the Left-Hand Path. I believe that this Infernal Tenet, if *fully* embraced, shall guide you to the transcendental fruits that you desire – the Satanist that applies the Infernal Tenet of Wisdom to their hellbound path shall enjoy the blessings that most souls only *dream* of receiving.

KNOWLEDGE IS DIVINITY

What image arises in your mind when you hear the word "occultist"? Is it the shadowy figure who, by moonlit altar, reads aloud the mysterious words of an ancient manuscript? Perhaps it is the witch who, beneath the willow's weeping boughs, serenades the frigid night with her ancestral spell – complete with black cats, cauldrons, and newt eyes? Of the millions that will read *The Satanic Philosopher*, I guarantee you that *every* reader's imagining of the occult shares in common this detail – the forbidden quest for transcendental knowledge and discovery.

All people, regardless of their religion, prejudices, fears, or dogma, associate the Left-Hand Path with *learning* – with knowledge of worlds hereafter and the pursuit of all truths forbidden to the lowly eyes of mortalkind – and this presumption is accurate. I do not believe there is *anything* more fundamental to the Left-Hand Path than the desire to unearth the long-forgotten truths meant not to be exhumed by the likes of humanity – except for the few amongst us who possess a timeless spirit and an affinity for the aberrant, the mysterious, and the supernatural.

These souls, like you and me, exist *far* beyond the multitude – we are cut from the same curious cloth by the shears of Atropos, forever fated to walk the overgrown roads of life and the Left-Hand Path in search of knowledge – in search of the secrets that were veiled by our forefathers and censured by the god-fearing tyrants of medieval millennia past. As a traditional Satanist, your pursuit of knowledge is your meaning of life – it is the fruit that begets all fruits – it is the Hesperian star that shall guide you on your journey to our kingdom of Hell, bestowing upon you *every* benediction that your heart desires.

What does it mean – the pursuit of knowledge? As a traditional Satanist, you might be asking yourself what you should be doing in your studies and faith, in order to attain the results that you seek from this Left-Hand Path. Is it simply a matter of reading old books? Are you expected to perform an invocation on a daily basis, wherein you interrogate the Devil Inquisition-style in hopes that he confesses to you some blasphemous secret? No – the answer is both simpler and more complex than any of these initial beliefs that you may have, regarding the pursuit of knowledge in traditional Satanism. In this religion, we regard knowledge and wisdom as two separate concepts – though entwined, they are not the same, and they must *both* be pursued by the Satanist. If I had to summarize the differences between the two, I would say that knowledge is the accumulation of information, and wisdom is the *application* of said information in a positive and constructive fashion.

Take a moment to reflect on that statement. If you disagree with my assertion, I ask that you consider this hypothetical scenario: You have the complete and total wealth of **all** knowledge at your disposal; anything you wish to know, you may now flip to a magical book page, and have it *perfectly* described to you in a way that you will infallibly and forever understand – this sounds like a great arrangement, right? Well, there is a catch – you can never act on the knowledge you have gained in any way, shape, or form – you cannot do anything *yourself* with the knowledge you have acquired, nor are you allowed to show another person your book or relay to them your expertise so that they may act on your behalf. What, now, do you believe the value of omniscient knowledge is when said knowledge cannot be used in an effective manner? It is absolutely *worthless*.

In traditional Satanism, we believe that knowledge is a catalyst for growth and that it is **not** indicative of growth itself – if the Satanist wishes to reap any benefit from their knowledge, then that knowledge *must* be applied in a way that improves their life or the lives of others. Once a person decides to apply their knowledge, *wisdom* shall bloom in its place. In theistic Satanism, we believe that wisdom is one of the most beautiful and invaluable blessings that a person can cultivate – second only to our natural born right to autonomy. For as long as you live and breathe, you will taste no nectar sweeter than that of wisdom – there exists no treasure, vice, power, or pleasure, on Earth or in Hell, that can eclipse the ambrosial benedictions of wisdom – it is *sublime*.

You may be wondering why Wisdom is one of our ministry's five Infernal Tenets, yet I have referred to the pursuit of *knowledge* rather than the pursuit of wisdom – allow me to explain. Though wisdom is *undoubtedly* more valuable than knowledge, the

Satanist cannot cultivate wisdom until they have a wealth of reliable knowledge at their disposal. The fruit of *any* harvest comes as a result of hard work, quality resources, and willpower – and cultivating wisdom works in the same way. You cannot smelt gold unless you have mined its ore, and you cannot taste the autumn apple unless its seed has first been sown – as well, you cannot refine knowledge into wisdom unless you already possess the knowledge that you wish to refine. It is for this reason that we, as theistic Satanists, pursue the crude resource that is knowledge – so that we have at our disposal the raw materials necessary to develop wisdom, which shall guide us to the transcendental power that we desire from both life itself and the Left-Hand Path.

Aside for autonomy, *nothing* is more cherished in traditional Satanism than wisdom – if autonomy is the heart of our religion, then wisdom is its sulfuric soul – they are two halves of the same coin, bound as one and *equally* necessary for the growth of the Satanist. It is a well-established belief throughout the world that traditional Satanism is synonymous with learning – with arcane knowledge, erudition, and diabolical enlightenment. In the absence of the pursuit of knowledge and the fostering of wisdom, traditional Satanism would cease to exist – it is an *irreplaceable* aspect of our faith's philosophy, and **no** occultist can justly call themselves a traditional Satanist if they disregard the pursuit of knowledge or the cultivation of wisdom. As a theistic Satanist, your ability to amass and apply arcane knowledge and sculpt from its ether an *extraordinary* life is as close to godliness as you will ever reach – there is an undeniable divinity in the pursuit of knowledge, and any traditional Satanist worth their fire would not need to be pressured into accepting this notion.

That said, since you have made it this far into *The Satanic Philosopher*, my guess is that I was correct when I suggested that you were cut from the same curious cloth as me – and, therefore, I do not need to convince you of the power of knowledge. If you are a theistic Satanist, your life and journey upon the Left-Hand Path should be an *endless* pursuit of knowledge and wisdom – there should never come a time in your mortal life where you stop learning, bettering yourself, or striving to reach new heights of self-empowerment. There is no expiry on being a better occultist or better human being – if air still fills your unhallowed lungs, you have no excuse to refuse the path of illumination – the path of eternal discovery, erudition, and transcendental evolution.

You are a traditional Satanist – like me, there is an *insatiable* hunger within you that never truly feels content – it murmurs, groans, and begrieves *every* second that passes where you do not unearth a new morsel of knowledge, or climb a higher summit of enlightenment. To the outside world, this would be regarded as a curse – but I believe it is the blessing that eclipses all blessings. Our world is a gruesome collage of *countless* dreary pieces – war, prejudice, malice, desolation – but there is *also* the plague of complacency. It is the fate that claimed most of the outside world – the trap of accepting one's current state of life or growth as "good enough." You are free to disagree with me, but I do not believe there is **any** room for the notion of "good enough" in the mind of the Satanist that recognizes their limitless potential as both a human and as a celebrant of our Lord Satan – as long as you walk this mortal Earth, you should *always* aim to conquer new ground in life and upon the Left-Hand Path that leads to Hell.

A THRONE OF GLASS

It is my belief that all malevolence is born from the wretched womb of *fear* – that **every** act of cruelty is motivated by the repressed fears and insecurities of those that commit said cruelties. If you disagree, take another look at the machinations of the crowd and the *ridiculous* excuses it uses to try and justify its mistreatment of others – xenophobia is covered up as patriotism and civic duty; the intolerance of religions that are not Catholicism or Christianity is thought of as upholding moral integrity, instead of crusaderism; the muzzling of free speech in order to coddle the emotionally feeble is masqueraded as civility and social progress, rather than a disregard for basic human rights. The crowd is nothing more than a frightened bully, aggressing the world in an attempt to create a false persona of strength so that nobody ever sees how fragile and fearful it *truly* is.

At every turn, the crowd *refuses* to admit that it is ruled by fear – it sugarcoats everything that it says, does, feels, and believes, veiling its vulnerabilities

197

and wickedness behind a plastic façade of warmth, empathy, and political correctness – it is a sinister, vaudevillian spectacle designed to earn the trust of the world while concealing its weakness behind an inconspicuous exterior. Of the many tricks that the crowd relies on to maintain this façade, its favorite is *misdirection* – to prevent you from noticing the crude stitching of its costume and the plot holes in its dreadful story, the crowd shall divert your focus to fictitious details, events, and villains so that you pay no attention to the malice spilling out from its seams – and there are few distractions as appealing to the crowd as the religion of traditional Satanism.

Our religion is the *perfect* scapegoat – a sacrificial lamb for the masses to pin upon their travesties and guilts so they do not have to take responsibility for being awful human beings. In a world enslaved by the edicts of God, it is *far* easier to blame Satanists or the Devil for everything that goes wrong in life, because nobody shall think twice or question your claims. I find a profound irony, in it all – the crowd blames Satan and his followers for the wickedness that plagues our world, yet, as far as I can tell, most acts of violence, cruelty, and wickedness that have been committed and documented over the past two millennia can be traced back to the heralds of God.

If you disagree with this belief, I challenge you to name a **single** war that has been fought in the name of Satan, at any point in humankind's history – you will never find one because it has never happened, yet you will find *hundreds* of wars and violent acts that have been waged in the name of God. For two thousand years, the Earth has wept and bled at the hands of those that use the word of God as a means to persecute others, all while blaming the Devil for the suffering that arises from their cruelties. Why? Because of *fear* – fear of what life would look like if the criers of God no longer controlled the world; fear of being held accountable for the cruelties that have been heaped upon others in the name of God; fear of admitting that God and his emissaries have contributed more suffering to humanity than Satan *ever* has; and, too, the fear of those that refuse the word of God in favor of the fire of our Lord Satan.

You see, the crowd will not admit it, but the hatred that it possesses for Satanists is *deeply* entrenched in fear – though the crowd likes to portray itself as strong and noble because it walks in the jaundiced light of Jesus Christ, I believe that the truth of the matter is less lionhearted and *far* sadder. It is quite obvious that the crowd fears Satanists – it does not understand why anyone would denounce the word of God in favor of Satan, and this confusion breeds a vitriolic cocktail of animosity, disgust, paranoia, anger, pietism, and you guessed it – *fear*. To those looking in from the outside, the Left-Hand Path of traditional Satanism is dangerous, mysterious, and frightening – an enigmatic blemish on a world that belongs to God and the neurotic lambs of his putrid flock – yet, despite their contempt for our religion, the crowd cannot help but to *also* remain intrigued.

Though the masses fear the Devil and his wayward followers, they *cannot* help but wonder – to ponder what aberrant and unholy things the Satanist down the street might get up to once the Sun sets and the city lies down to slumber. For millennia, the crowd has conjured up campfire stories and fables about devil worshippers – about the *unspeakable* things that we may do under the covers of night, when the prying eyes of our neighbors are no longer awake and watching our every move – drinking the blood of virgins, sacrificing animals, eating children, and selling our soul to Satan, just to name a few of the most popular tales told by the murmuring masses.

As you can see, these legends and superstitions do not paint traditional Satanists accurately, nor in the kindest light – why, then, does the crowd *continue* to maintain interest and fascination in what it is we do? If the world reviles us so deeply, then why do we remain an excitingly taboo topic of speculation for the prim and proper cogs of society? If you dig through the cliché images, symbols, and allegories that our religion is associated with – the black cats, cauldrons, altars, spellbooks, and rituals – you will find this core element that rouses both fascination and fear from the crowd: *our pursuit of knowledge*.

The Satanist's pursuit of knowledge is at the heart of *every* legend, fear, and folklore that has afflicted our religion for over two thousand years – from the hysteria of medieval days, crusades, and the Salem executions of the 1690s, to the Satanic Panic of the 1980s and the hyperbole of the 21st century – there is no superstition surrounding traditional Satanism that fails to reflect the crowd's fright and curiosity, regarding the Satanist's quest for knowledge. You see, as outsiders looking in, the masses do not have context for the sacrilegious sights they see when it comes to traditional Satanism – all that is apparent to them is that we practice magic, despise the word of God, and worship Satan. In order to make sense of our blasphemous ways, the masses turn to what *most* outsiders turn to when attempting to grasp an aberrant concept – they begin to speculate, hoping that clarity arises from what crumbs of insight they may possess and the hypotheses they have created.

What ends up happening, though, is not the growth of clarity but the cultivation of misinformation and the heightening of *fear*. As the god-fearing masses attempt to vivisect and understand the nature of the Satanist, what meager crumbs of insight the crowd might have *initially* possessed get filtered through many layers of prejudice and paranoia – eventually leading to the invention of superstitions and horror stories instead of anything that resembles the truth.

Over the past two thousand years, the **only** morsel of accurate information the crowd has managed to piece together is this – that the Satanist *relentlessly* pursues transcendental knowledge. With this small window of insight into the dark and ethereal world of traditional Satanism, the crowd tries to fill in the remaining blanks and missing details that surround our faith. It is at this point where the masses begin to assume the worst, speculating over what strange and *ghoulish* acts the Satanist *must* be committing on behalf of the Devil, in exchange for the infernal knowledge they seek – sacrificing animals, killing virgins, selling one's soul – you know the classics.

It is a complex question – why does the crowd fear the Satanist's pursuit of knowledge? Of the myriad reasons why the masses shriek and spin their scary stories of soul-selling devil worshippers, I believe the most ubiquitous reason is this: the *implications* of the Satanist's pursuit of knowledge. You see, in a world enslaved by the tyranny of God, nothing is more frightening than disobedience – than *defying* the word of God in favor of Satan, and seeking his forbidden knowledge. Once this blasphemy of the Satanist is met with the crowd's lack of insight into what the Satanist does behind closed doors, fear is free to bubble forth – the floodgates of superstition opening wide for all matter of *fantastical* legends, myths, and fables to spill out – and that is precisely how we ended up with so many sensational stories surrounding our faith, over the past two millennia.

What, *then*, might our pursuit of knowledge imply in the god-fearing mind of the crowd? Beyond the folktales of soul-selling, sacrifices, and butchering animals, there is one core implication that *cripples* the masses with absolute terror – that God may not *actually* be all-powerful nor all-knowing. If God is all-knowing, then why would people be willing to weather two thousand years of subjugation, so that they may inherit the knowledge of Satan? If God is omniscient and all-powerful, why is it that Satan holds such a presence in our world? If God is truly all-powerful, he would be able to extinguish Satan, his celebrants, and our religion with the snap of a finger – therein, ending the eons-old war between Heaven and Hell. But he does not do this – instead, the masses cover up God's frailties and failures by claiming that he "allows" Satan to exist as a test of humanity's faith. If this is true, it is proof that God is little more than a deified psychopath that abuses the trust and vulnerabilities of his followers for his own entertainment – if false, it proves that God is not only washed-up and weak, but that he is also a *deceiver* – does that sound familiar? For over two thousand years, the Church has defamed the Devil by referring to *him* as "the deceiver" – yet, at least from my perspective, this title is far more fitting of God than Satan – perhaps the masses already know this, though, and it is all just another cunning game of misdirection – of masquerading fear as strength.

As you go forward in life and upon the Left-Hand Path of traditional Satanism, you will encounter an *unfathomable* degree of opposition from the lambs of God – to you, your religion, and your pursuit of transcendental knowledge. In the pious eyes of the masses, you will be viewed as an *abomination* – a spiritual car crash of sorts, too grotesque to look at yet too captivating to look away from – an atrocity that should not be, but is. The crowd will not know how to explain your existence, so it will do what it has done for over two thousand years – it will turn to speculation, substituting clarity and truth for the superstitions of medieval days. The masses, then, will frighten themselves with the figments of their runaway imaginations – like children telling ghost

205

stories on a dark and stormy night, the holy hordes of God will rile themselves up with rumors of your wickedness – the Satanist living in their little slice of suburban Heaven, making deals with the Devil.

You must remember that the pulse of this wretched world is tethered to the venae cavae of God – even if you *quietly* embrace your beliefs as a traditional Satanist, the world **will** notice, and it **will** respond vehemently – with vitriol, condemnation, loathing, ridicule, and fear. As I have discussed throughout *The Satanic Philosopher,* this is the discriminatory price that we must pay in exchange for our pursuit of knowledge and the expression of our faith – the cruelty of a holier-than-thou world that persecutes *any* soul who dares rebuke the tyranny of God. As a traditional Satanist, *this* is your cross to bear – to weather the craven masses of Christ that will resort to all manner of incivility and barbarity in order to mask their inveterate fear of you, your beliefs, and your pursuit of forbidden knowledge – *everything* that you hold dear as an apostle of our Lord Satan.

THE ALCHEMY OF KNOWLEDGE

What is it that I mean when I refer to the pursuit of *transcendental* knowledge? How is it any different than everyday knowledge – the kind that you may acquire through books, life experiences, or formal education? Is it not true that *all* knowledge should be pursued? Allow me to explain. I believe that all knowledge **is** valuable, but some knowledge more than others – like a dazzling sapphire, the value of knowledge is not implicit but, rather, it depends on a multitude of factors. What is the weight? How is the clarity? Are there any imperfections that would cloud the beauty of the jewel before you? Like any other treasure or artifact, knowledge, *too*, varies in value based on a *plethora* of factors – its accuracy, relevancy, and potency being the criteria by which most knowledge is assessed by the average person.

While these factors *are* essential for appraising the value of knowledge, knowledge is worthless if it is unapplicable – as I discussed in the "Knowledge is Divinity" subchapter of *The Satanic Philosopher*, knowledge is only as valuable as its potential to be used in a way that leads to quantifiable growth and change in a meaningful direction. If the knowledge in question is trivial, or if the knower does not use their knowledge in a productive manner, then said knowledge will not contribute to the betterment of one's life. As traditional Satanists, we are not here to acquire knowledge so that it may collect dust on the shelf or serve as a bragging point at the cocktail lounge – we are here to amass knowledge that will allow us to change our lives and the world *forever*.

So – what *are* the differences between knowledge and *transcendental* knowledge? The short version is that knowledge pertains to the material, physical world, and transcendental knowledge refers to the metaphysical – it is an alchemical duality, of sorts. If you hope to ever attain *true* empowerment from our faith of traditional Satanism, you must pursue both knowledge and its transcendental variety with equal enthusiasm. How, then, do you recognize the differences between the two during your practices, studies, and everyday life? Why is it essential that you *equally* pursue both types of knowledge, even if you believe that your unique goals in life or upon the Left-Hand Path do not require one or the other?

Think back to my previous allegory of the book of eternal knowledge – how useless its contents were once you realized you could never utilize what you read from its gilded pages. Well, this *also* becomes the case when one form of knowledge is forsaken for the other – how can you ever manifest physical change with the knowledge you amass unless you, first, cultivate the emotional, mental, and spiritual sagacity needed to achieve such a Herculean task? The pursuit of knowledge primarily pertains to the world around you and your place in it – how things work, how people work, and how you can manifest your vision of an idyllic life amidst the madness of this mortal Earth. On the other hand, the pursuit of *transcendental* knowledge concerns all things that belong to the intangible – the mind, emotions, and spirit, as well as the metaphysical – everything that exists *beyond* what may be seen, touched, or heard.

Okay, so we know now that knowledge pertains to the material world, and transcendental knowledge to the immaterial – how, then, do we pursue either? Though it may initially seem complex, I guarantee you it is *far* easier than it appears – the answer lies in your embodiment of our five Infernal Tenets. As a traditional Satanist, adhering to these tenets shall give you a clear understanding of what you should do, avoid, and prioritize in order to have a fruitful experience in your faith. The Satanist that adheres to the five Infernal Tenets will never have a reason to question what steps come next in their journey upon the Left-Hand Path, for they will *always* have the tools required to see these steps for themselves.

When I first created our five Infernal Tenets many years ago, I did so meticulously, with cohesion and synergy foremost in mind: the tenet of Clarity shall allow you to see *everything* accurately, without the fog of fear and doubt clouding your judgment. The ability to clearly assess your life, your dreams, and your place in this cataclysmic world will allow you to recognize where you are in relation to the idyllic life you wish to live – and, because you have seen the alternative of living an unfulfilling life, the fire of Devotion shall be lit beneath your ass, inspiring you to nurture your innermost potential so that you may bring to life your *every* dream. Once you have determined how and why you wish to change your life, you must begin your journey – the god-fearing masses will attempt to slow your progress at every turn, but they *will* fail. The world shall never break you, for you shall never surrender to its malevolent tempests – and with your defiance, the essences of Resilience and Autonomy will mature within your spirit, making you ever more unconquerable by the world. And Wisdom – with the other four Infernal Tenets already emboldening you, you become free to build upon what you have begun to create – your vision of an idyllic life, inspired and made possible through your *continued* pursuit of knowledge in its binate forms – the physical and the transcendental.

Pay careful attention to my choice of words – your *continued* pursuit of knowledge. You see, the truth is that the knowledge you pursue is all around you, awaiting your discovery – it is hiding in *everything* you do, feel, witness, suffer, and experience, from the magical to the mundane. In every circumstance that life presents – every tragedy, fortune, disaster, creation, failure, and achievement – an abundance of knowledge awaits your discovery, provided that you are observant enough to notice it and receptive enough to accept it. Oftentimes, people do not look deeply into the inner workings of life – they simply welcome the good and lament the bad, discrediting the possibility of there being something further for them to learn from the happenings at hand. It is an unpopular opinion of mine, but I believe that there is *always* something more to learn – even from the worst fates that a person can suffer. The things that happen to us in life are not static events, but rather, they are *catalysts* – liquid, malleable, and shapable opportunities for us to turn tragedies into triumphs.

This concept of transformation is at the heart of *all* occultism – *Solve et Coagula*. At the core of every study and faith upon the Left-Hand Path, you shall find this concept of transmogrifying one thing into another, in pursuit of power – lead into gold, water into wine, life into Death, and Death into life. This notion of eternal transformation is a principle upon which *countless* studies have built their foundation throughout humankind's sordid history – alchemy, psychology, witchcraft, Hermeticism, Wicca, and, yes – traditional Satanism. Though every study has its own interpretation of what this principle means, I believe that psychology is the root of it all – how the practitioner interprets and transcends the many horrors of life, turning the ugliness and misfortune of the world into opportunities for metamorphosis.

As a traditional Satanist, this is the greatest tool in your arsenal – the ability to recognize, reduce, and transform the happenings of life into opportunities to attain knowledge and, in turn, foster the growth of wisdom. It is the telltale sign of a sagacious soul to be able to turn adversity into advantage – to turn even the most painful, harrowing, and *insufferable* tempests of life into fuel for growth. The mind that can always find a means to enlighten and empower itself despite the chaos of the world around it shall become of the gods – *brilliant*, and unconquerable like the ebon gates of Hell. To be able to transform everything that life throws at you into a means of learning, growing, and bettering yourself is a form of mortal *divinity* – it is the alchemy of knowledge.

THE DEVIL'S TEMPTATION

If I asked you to think of *any* story from the Bible that speaks about the Devil, odds are you will think of Lucifer's fall from Heaven or the temptation of Adam and Eve – both stories being *equally* crucial to understanding God's tyranny and the heroism of our Lord Satan. However, despite the religious and historical significance of these two tales, the world remains oblivious to what they *really* prove – the masses believe that these stories depict the Devil's wickedness, when, in reality, they illustrate God's sadistic, cruel, and Machiavellian nature. If you do not believe me, that is okay – settle down for story time with Reverend Cain, and allow me to explain.

It is the origin story of humankind's creation – the tale of Adam and Eve. In the beginning of time and space within *this* universe, a narcissistic deity who would be known as God began to shape everything into existence – and this process would take seven days. On the sixth day of creation, God shaped his magnum opus abomination from the clay and soot of Earth – *a human being.* This human was a man, and his name was Adam. In the wake of giving life to Adam, God created an everlasting sanctuary for him to live in – a paradise known as the Garden of Eden. Then, from the rib of Adam, God fashioned a *second* human – a woman named Eve. Together, Adam and Eve lived a pinioned life of marital bliss within the Garden of Eden – but this came with its share of rules, tests, and stipulations. Above every limitation that God set for Adam and Eve, one was to be heeded as the most crucial to follow – **never** eat the fruit from the tree of forbidden knowledge.

Without an option to refuse, Adam and Eve agreed to obey the word and rules of God – after all, it felt like a small price to pay in exchange for living an idyllic life. As time stretched onwards, the genesis couple enjoyed their rapturous life together, eating figs and dancing in the sunlight – they suffered no troubles, pains, or plights, for they lived within the predacious eye of God – their oh-so caring creator-turned-captor – the warden of the Garden of Eden. As the story goes, Adam and Eve continued to live in bliss until one day, they felt a darkness – it clung thickly to the air, and the dew – it dripped from the forest's canopy like a torrent of gloom, and a sense of *quenchless* dread began to fill the two doe-eyed lovers. On one ill-fated day in the Garden of Eden, Eve gazed upon the tree of knowledge with a sense of curiosity – then, *bewitched*, she approached the tree to look closer at the ambrosial fruits that hung from its boughs – and a serpent slithered out from its verdant leaves, confessing his name to be Satan.

Though frightened, Eve, too, was *fascinated* – and she listened as the Devil revealed to her all manner of *blasphemous* truths regarding God, his tyranny, and the fruit of forbidden knowledge. Then, Satan tempted Eve into eating the fruit of knowledge and defying the rule of God – and Eve agreed, because she had *finally* seen the true nature of God as a liar, and a tyrant. In that fateful moment, Eve reached out her pallid hand and grasped the brightest, most nectarous fruit that hung from the tree of forbidden knowledge – Eve, then, raised that ambrosial fruit to her tender lips and sank her teeth into it – at last, defying the word of God. In a flash that seemed to last a lifetime, Eve looked upon **all** truths that had been concealed from her and Adam – horrified and excited all the same, she rushed over to Adam and encouraged him to *also* consume the fruit – and he did, therein receiving the same revelations that just moments prior had frightened and enraptured Eve.

That evening, God approached Adam and Eve and asked them about their day – at which point, they confessed to God that they disobeyed him and had eaten from the tree of forbidden knowledge. Filled with rage, disappointment, and a bruised ego, God condemned Adam and Eve – original sin was born, and Death would now find not only Adam and Eve but *every* instance of mortal life that did and would ever exist – every plant, animal, and human being was, *therein*, predestined to a lifetime of pain, fear, and suffering. As God threw a tantrum and cursed his now-sovereign creations, Adam and Eve were exiled from the Garden of Eden – at which point, humanity was pre-damned for all eternity unless it *promised* to remain forever obedient to God's rule.

What a Hell of a story, am I right? I think it is a bit of an overreaction to condemn not only two people but an entire *species* to eternal pain, suffering, and damnation all for eating a fucking apple – but what can I say? God has a long, hideous history of being cruel and unhinged. Though God's instability does not surprise me, it *does* frighten me to see how the masses respond to the story of Adam and Eve – the general reaction being along the lines of, "and that is why you must *obey* God," rather than, "what the Hell is *wrong* with God?" Honestly – my religious beliefs aside, any rational person can find a *million* deranged plot holes in the story of Adam and Eve.

Why would God create a paradise for his **only** two human beings, only to plant a tree in it whose fruit was forbidden from being consumed? Why would God, then, impart the knowledge of good and evil into this tree – why would he not simply keep it for himself, locked away within some angelic library? Why would God set the punishment so high for the consumption of the fruit of knowledge – why was eternal pain, fear, suffering, and Death for not only Adam and Eve, but *all* mortal life and the future of humankind the **only** possible punishment he could think of? Unfortunately, we are nearing the end of our time together with *The Satanic Philosopher*, so I cannot venture *too* far into my opinions regarding the holes in this story and my beliefs regarding the instabilities of God – we would be here for another 220 pages, if I had that much time left to speculate.

I believe that, at its core, the tale of Adam and Eve demonstrates *precisely* what I have discussed over the course of *The Satanic Philosopher* – the fear of knowledge falling into the hands of those that have denounced the tyranny of God. Of course, the god-fearing masses did not yet exist back in the days of Adam and Eve – but the principles with which they persecute Satanists, and the rest of the world *today* are those that even the all-mighty God used against the first humans he ever created – almost as if there were clear signs since the very beginning that God was a tyrant, and we should have seen his brutality coming from a mile away. But we did not – either that, or the first sycophants of God chose to ignore these signs since they believed themselves to be on the right side of religious history – a delusion that the masses carry with confidence to this very day.

So – what can we learn from the infamous story of Adam and Eve? Well, *a lot* – foremost, that God is a tyrant, the Devil has always had our best interest at heart, and that the messengers of God fear few things more than knowledge in the hands of those that have rejected God's so-called authority. These lessons may *also* be found in the story of Lucifer's exile, and most other tales in the Bible – even those without any mentioning of demons, Hell, or Satan. As well, the story of Adam and Eve teaches us that the pursuit of knowledge is supported by Satan and reviled by God – the reason being that Satan wants us to be autonomous and powerful, and God wants us to remain subservient and weak – this makes the Devil your ally, and God, a *plague* to your growth, enlightenment, independence, and potential in life.

I could not give a shit less about what the accepted narrative is – God is **not** the good guy and Satan is **not** the root of the world's problems. When left to his own devices, God *always* resorts to his old bag of tricks: he plays mind games with his followers by giving them impossible tests of "faith," which often require them to defy their human nature and do *terrible* things – murdering their own children, starving themselves, forgoing all forms of comfort and pleasure, etc. Once they fail, God will retaliate

221

with acts of *overwhelming* violence, barbarity, and sadistic glee – then, watching from afar, the crowd points and screams, "look – look at what the Devil did! Repent in the name of Christ, and you shall be spared from this suffering!" All the while, God and his cronies are the ones spreading the lion's share of the world's suffering – the masses misdirect you with the hand that points at Satan, all while carving through the world with the other hand in the name of God – it is all just a cover of smoke and mirrors, and you will **not** fall victim to this archaic charade.

The story of Adam and Eve is a grim one, to those who are not blinded by heavenly fanaticism – there are **zero** commendable points to God's side of this story, and *any* soul that finds heroism in its lessons instead of disgust and horror is a person that I want no affiliation with. If you were to find any valuable lesson in the story of Adam and Eve, I hope that it is this – God is **not** your friend, and he wants you to remain as servile and clueless as is possible. The Devil, on the other hand – the Devil shall abet your pursuit of knowledge, because **he** knows the value of wisdom, and autonomy – after all, it was he that risked his life and reputation in pursuit of not only his own freedom to thrive beyond God's senseless limitations, but for humankind's – for *our* freedom to live, pray, govern, and grow freely, and without the suffocating shadow of God eclipsing our *every* finite flicker of mortal life – the Devil is our savior.

As a traditional Satanist, your ambitions will likely align with those of our Lord Satan – the pursuit of knowledge will become your polestar, and nobody shall disrupt your journey – not the crowd, not this god-forsaken world, and not even God himself. As a beacon of Hell on Earth, you shall transcend the pitiful masses – those that surrender any morsel of moral integrity they may have to God, so that they *might* be spared from his vicious crusade. Though it may sound impossible, or too difficult for you to achieve – you **can** achieve it. Through your pursuit of knowledge and your exemplification of our five Infernal Tenets, **nothing** on Earth is beyond your ability to achieve. You are a celebrant of our Lord Satan, and, in your devotion to its attainment, his nature may becometh your nature – his resilience, clarity, autonomy, and, *too*, his diabolical wisdom.

THE SATANIC PHILOSOPHER

In your hands, you hold the fruit of my life's work, and devotion – *The Satanic Philosopher*. This is a bittersweet moment for me, as I type the last words of my magnum opus manuscript – it is impossible for me to describe this feeling of tying the bow on and sending off into the world my dearest and most prized creation – but it is *both* somber and sublime.

The past half-decade of me amassing experiences, musing, writing, and *finally* stitching together this manuscript has been and will forever be one of the proudest moments of my mortal life. I am honored to have had this opportunity, and I believe that this book shall accomplish *tremendous* feats in life and upon the Left-Hand Path that leads to our kingdom of Hell – this book shall change the world, forever.

With *The Satanic Philosopher,* I have attempted to right the many wrongs that have tarnished our faith of traditional Satanism for more than two thousand god-fearing years – the hysteria, superstitions, and xenophobic hyperbole that has been perpetrated by the fear-mongering masses of a world that delights in the sallow light of God – the tyrant of all tyrants, and the patron saint of carnage to those that live by his despotic word. The masses – that dreary, cruel, and mindless multitude of God that trudges across the loam of Earth like a patchwork abomination of crusaderism, delusion, and wickedness. The crowd of God is, in my eyes, little more than a teratoma appendage of hatred, fear, and malevolence, glued together with egoism and a false sense of morality.

As a traditional Satanist, you likely already know that God is a pitiless con artist – a streetside trader, peddling the snake oil of salvation under the threat of pain and suffering if you refuse his offer. There are few things redeemable about God and his little lambs – though I have known many honorable and respectable Christians throughout my life, *most* of them have fulfilled the stereotype that I have come to know and experience firsthand as both a Satanic minister and an ordinary citizen. That said, even in the malevolence of the god-fearing crowd, there is powerful insight to be reaped – above all else, that your faith as a traditional Satanist shall mark you a leper in the eyes of a world that dances to the war drums of God – the tyrant-king of this pious Earth.

As theistic Satanists, the odds were stacked against us from the very beginning – errant, blasphemous, and uncontrollable. We know what God is capable of doing to his detractors, and still – *we persist*. We do not fear the will or wickedness of his lambs, for the will of the Devil is *greater* – and so, *too*, is the fire that burns within every apostle of his scriptural reign. As a traditional Satanist, the fire that flames within your brimstone heart shall *always* outblaze the ashen light of God – and, too, your willful soul shall *always* weather the tempests of life and those that would call themselves the heralds of Heaven.

– Rev. Cain

OTHER PUBLICATIONS

The Infernal Gospel

The Goetia Devils

The Goetia Hymns

Ars Diabolica

Ars Animarum

Ars Aeterna

Ars Sanguinea

Ars Exitialis

The Abyssal Bible – Coming Soon

The Hierophant of Hell – Coming Soon

You may find us on Facebook, as well as on Etsy, where we offer our world-renowned demonological grimoires, occult antiques, and *numerous* Left-Hand Path oddities.

For business inquiries, please use the messaging feature on Etsy and contact us directly – if your inquiries regard wholesale purchase of our paperback books, we cannot directly assist you – it **is** something that we offer, but it must be done via Amazon KDP's business services, and we cannot facilitate the process in any meaningful way.

Facebook: @TheInfernalCircle

Etsy: TheInfernalCircle